Dear Reader:

I wrote this journal as part of my process of healing the grief of losing my oldest daughter through rebellion and estrangement. I did not try be politically, religiously, or emotionally correct; I just wrote to be, period. In life, I embrace the "let and let live," philosophy and I am hoping you, my reader, will do the same for me. Thank you for being part of my journey and I hope you write about yours.

Bailey Larroquette

"Don't let anyone tell you

your prayers aren't heard;

Because you don't speak the language.

Because you don't live on the land.

Because you don't carry a pipe.

Because you don't have tobacco.

Because you aren't wearing a skirt.

Because you are not heterosexual enough.

Everyone is free to pray.

In the end, only Creator gets to decide

Which prayers will be answered

so PRAY."

Author Unknown.

Posted on the psychiatric hospital wall.

December 24th, 2019

Dear Riley;

I am writing to you from the pschiatric hospital. Losing you again is a big part of the problem; why I crashed so hard. That and all those cruel, evil emails that far surpassed disrespect of a parent but whatever— I am writing this to wash my side of the window clean. You are an adult now and your are responsible for your side of the view.

How I miss you, my beautiful girl. I wish you had always felt loved by me and I'm sorry you didn't.

I remember one rainy day in K____, we were driving in my 1968 Crysler Windsor and you piped up from the back seat; "Mom, the rain is giggling on the roof." And another poignant moment was when we were walking by a church with a cross on the roof and you pointed to it and announced: "look. That's where God died."

Your artwork is just amazing. Someone showed me your etsy store and some facebook stuff. The beadwork is breath taking. Loved the Barbie necklace. I saw the painting of a rainbow across your desk and I remembered how your Dad and I planned on him painting a mural across my bedroom furniture but it didn't happen. Now you are performing our unfinished artwork. Very interesting.

Your father could also doodle and it turned out better than my best intentions, haha.

Christmas Joke: Three wise women would have asked directions, cleaned the stable, baked a casserole, and there would be peace on earth. Ha ha. Or not.

I pray for you alot. God must have big plans for you little girlie. The bigger His blessing the more He inspires me to pray, it seems. Big Daddy takes me—His little girl to work with Him as He works on my little girl-you.

Love, Mom

_____

_____

_____

"I alone know the plans I have for you, plans to bring you prosperity and not disaster, plans to bring about the future you hope for." Jeremiah 29:11 (GNB)

December 25th, 2019

Dear Riley;

Merry Christmas! That was your favourite Bible verse.

I have never forgotten the day you were born. You were soooo tiny and your skin felt like the finest silk. I was so full of love for you I wondered how it was even possible to love someone that much. I knew then that I would die for you if need be—just never realized I would one day be suicidal over your cruel words, racial rejection and total separation.

I do not even remember when exactly we stopped talking, only that even getting along never seemed like getting along. You bombard me with communication and demands for attention, usually over text, and then when I can't resolve your question or don't give enough attention you go ape-snake-canary-crackers (my term for ballistic) and cut me off. Usually with the usual barrage of verbal abuse: "you were a horrible f-ing mother, you didn't do right by me, da dee dah." I am sorry you feel like you had such a horrible upbringing while I feel like I did the best with what I had at the time. Today I feel like I could do better but I am not being allowed to do that and while I know today does not make up for yesterday, today is all we have. It's all anyone has.

Yesterday your Grandfather admitted they have an address for you. So this summer when Rachel and I go up for their 50th wedding anninversary I will pack up your baby books and trinkets and take them there to be sent on to you, as per demand via the grapevine on balertwine.

Hopefully you will get to know Grandma and Grandpa before they go. They are 70 and 73. Wowsers. But I understand the causcasion side of the family tree is extremely secondary to you. Oooo no bitterness there.

Google "The LaLoche Project: a documentary on the remote Saskatchewan Village," a university student did the work and I believe at least one of your relatives is starred.

You were so particular when you bought your seed beads for crafting, they had to be from the store near W. that looks like Green Gables, remember?

One of your school teachers used to call you;

"Persnickety." It's another word for picky.

This is our third Christmas apart and I have missed three of your birthdays. I am going to start stock piling gifts for when I see you again.

Love Mom

_____

_____

_____

"The world can be a very unforgiving place so never apoligize for who you are." Line from an actress on Days of Our Lives.

"The world needs more people like who God designed you to be."-Unknown

December 26th, 2019

Dear Riley;

Out on a pass today, I gathered what is left of your baby clothes and packed it up. All I am keeping is the negatives and a few loose photos. Rachel will have to help me sort the few crumbs of artwork remaining from your childhoods so you get the right stuff.

Your dad used to add an "s" to words that did not really require them, like "furnitures," and how he tried to sell his "arts." I gave up trying to correct him.

Another thing he used to say is "I sez," when he was quoting himself having told someone off.

When you girls were growing up and we could not decide on a movie we would throw our choices into a pillowcase and then draw a V.H.S. movie out. I miss those days.

I am glad you inherited your fotah's (fathers) dog. What a dorky mutt. I bet you cracks you up many times a day. It's like he is constantly telling jokes the way he clowns around.

It's HARD to live without you girl. Oh I know I've said things in the past I shouldn't have but I miss you so much. What parent does not ever succumb to exhaustion? At least I can open this diary and talk to you. It's something anyways. (Another word from your pop: anyways).

Anyway, bye for now,

Love Mom

_____

_____

_____

"Stop your crying and wipe away your tears. All that you have done for your children will not go unrewarded; they will return from the enemy's land. There is hope for your future; your children will come back home." Jeremiah 31:16,17 (GNB).

December 27th, 2019

Dear Riley;

In ladie's Bible study the leader said when she was talking about all "our prodigals;" (wayward children)"We are to see them returning." Sometimes I can, other times I can't.

I am back in the hospital, roomed with a tiny blonde and an aboriginal girl, and it reminds me of you and Rachel. We all display symptoms of P.T.S.D. And we are all mothers without our children. Mine are grown theirs are in the care of others until their mothers get what they need here.

The flowered wall paper in here is enough to blur one's vision, and the old, empty hospital that used to house looks just like Parliament Hill. It is also said to be haunted...a bunch of patients want to sneak out and creep around the building but I declined the invitation. How counterproductive— when you are already haunted by flashbacks on a good day.

At times this experience is more like a bizarre vacation with the hot tub, swimming pool, crafts and ceremics. How will they get rid of me, haha.

For the most part, we are all friends here, and why not? Everyone here has had a fallout with mental health and I wish society knew it can happen to anyone. No one is immune to a breakdown.

Someone said "...People with mental illness, are, I find, among the wisest, kindest and sanest people I have ever met." I find this atmosphere more loving and accepting than alot of churches I have been to, and that is beyond a tad sad. We must however, make an effort not to judge the judgemental, for that is still mental. Haha.

I'll talk to you real soon.

Love Mom

"It is wisdom that has faced the pain caused by parents, spouse, family, friends, colleagues, business associates, and has truly forgiven them and acknowledged with unexpected compassion that these people are neither angels nor devils, but only human."
-Brennan Manning (deceased).

December 28th, 2019

Dear Riley;

If I concentrate really hard, I can hear your voice and even hear you clear your throat.

I pray for you every day; that God would bring you back to himself, that he would deliver you of evil, and that you would hear his voice again like that summer you were baptized. Even if you don't come back to me it is imperative that you come back to God.

I remember getting a flat on my way to pick you up from Bible camp and missing your baptism. Arrrrgh. You went ahead with it anyway; "it's what God told me to do."

You know, hatred and bitterness are like drinking poison and hoping the other guy dies, and mental illness has its root in the inability to give and/or forgive. Interesting.

One day I hope you embrace all of your heritages, not just one. Do you remember how you asked me once what nationality you were since you came from a German Mennonite and a French Aboriginal? And we came up with Germindianite...which left out the smidgen of french. Your dad was a descendant of King Louie and he was sure proud of it. I am not sure how many "greats," are on the list.

With your Mom being from a town called "La Crete," and your pop being from "La Loche," you are from "La-la Land," haha. I used to bug you about that.

When you were a toddler, your favourite bedtime story was the book;"Julie and the Puppy." And you used to say;"read to woo, read to woo,"when you wanted me to read to you. So cute.

One day you will do great things for God.

Miss you. Love you lots.

Mom

"Do all the good you can, in all the places you can, by all the means you can, in all the ways you can, in all the places you can, at all the times you can, to all the people you can." –John Wesley

"Be kind, for everyone you meet is fighting a hard battle." –Plato

December 29th, 2019

Dear Riley;

Sometimes I wish reproduction didn't even happen until all the ducks and stars were aligned just right, but then which one of us would be here?

The world's ugliest ankle bracelet is about to be made with your name on it. Wow do I suck at beading, lol. But it will say Riley Waneetah Burdette in clumsy bead lettering.

Read all of Jeremiah 29 sometime, it is God's promise to your people. One day, perhaps, you will rewrite the scriptures for the aboriginals; a First Nations Standard Version. And maybe you will design a healing model of their ultimate rehabilitation.

You aren't walking with God right now but He has never left you. I hope he gives you a hug from me often.

It is sure fun to tuck little gifts into your baby memorabilia. There are three years of holidays gone now. Three birthdays, three Valentine's Days, three Easters, Thanksgiving Days, and three Christmases.

The pain of losing a child is almost unbearable. God knows what that is like and He walks me through this wilderness journey in the tangled valley until you come back. We need each other more than you think.

All my love,

Mom

_____

_____

_____

"An unhealed person can find offense in pretty much anything someone does.

A healed person understands that the actions of others have absolutely nothing to do with them.

Each day you get to decide which one you will be."

December 30th, 2019

Dear Riley;

Should I just write with straight whiteout and skip the middle part- the attempt at writing? Lol.

Do you know how hard it is to hold a one sided conversation, haha.

I wish I had always been kind. I was not raised with a silver spoon in my mouth, it was more like a rusty fork and there are things that go along with that. Then I had two kids and raised them in colossal poverty alone with no help at all. It sounds like excuses but I am not making any. This is all fact.

I am sorry I seemed to favour Rachel over you. She was simply the easier child to raise in hard times. It isn't that I loved her more or that I love her more now. A parent's love for a child is unconditional. Said every crappy parent ever, haha.

You girls practically raised yourselves. I had to be Mom and Dad too, husband and wife...I like to think

I wound you up and pointed you but you brought yourself and your sister up. So don't worry about the kind of parent you will be, you already know. You have experience.

I was neglectful, stuck in my own emotional pain, and reactive alot of the time. I also like to think I did some things right, and its imperative you find something good in me to be grateful for for the sake of your own healing. Gratitude helps overcome obstacles. There is still a magnet on my fridge that says:"Get rich quick- count your blessings."

No one can apologize or make amends forever, and I won't. At some point you either forgive or you don't. I hope you can forgive me one day instead of this negative relationship between us becoming your entire identity. No one has the power to change the past and even God won't...He says He is "The Great I Am," not "The great I was."

Anne Frank said;"I don't think then, of all the misery, but of the beauty that still remains."

Love, Mom

_____

_____

_____

Broken Dreams

As children bring

their broken toys to us

with tears for us to mend,

I brought my broken

dreams to God

because he was my friend.

But then instead of leaving him

in peace to work alone

I hung around

and tried to help

with ways that were my own.

At last I snatched them back

and cried: "How could you be so slow?!"

"My child," he said,

"What could I do? You never did let go."

Author Unknown, poem taken from a book by author Crying Wind.

"The truth will always set you free of the people who can't handle the truth."–Me

"If we all knew exactly what the other person thought none of us would be friends."–Unknown

"What you think of me is none of my business."–Terry Cole-Whittaker

December 31st, 2019

Dear Riley;

Happy New Year!

And what? I spelled one of your names wrong on the bracelet. It should be Waneetah with an h. Maybe I can get some whiteout on that, haha. Wait til you see the keychain I tried to make, it will prove you did not inherit your talent from me, lol. Well maybe the creativity.

Still praying for healing for our relationship everytime I think of you, which is alot.

Are you going straight to the top and getting your P.H.D. in social work I wonder. You certainly have the brains to do it. Oh, you were always so smart! Wise beyond your years.

How I long for a time capsule so I could bring you back as a little girl and hold you again. Let you mess up the house and your hair and leave it that way.

When you were still a toddler, you and I used to make "button pictures." We glued sewing notions to cardboard or construction paper and hung them on the dining room wall after the glue had dried. Man, did we come up with some good stuff, I tell you. There are pictures of the pictures somewhere.

Well look at this, no whiteout. Woot woot.

Outside is a winter wonderland, and I should know, coming from almost northernmost Alberta. The first time I walked outside of the hospital I promptly got lost. This is a big place in a small world...years ago I worked as a caregiver for a quadriplegic man who had been a night watchman here and was struck by a car.

During my career as a care aide, I learned some senior swears: "Good night!" "Heavens to Betsy!" and "Honest to Pete!" All exclamations. Being a hopeless romantic, I can't help but wonder if Pete and Betsy ever met.

So I have spent Christmas in the nuthouse. Rachel and I had some time together in the foyer by the scarred old piano and vending machine on Christmas Eve.

Today I told doctor A: "you gotta lemme outta here, this place is driving me nuts!" He laughed and said; "Me too, somedays."

I tinkered on the old wooden upright piano out in the main area, but I am not a good candidate for piano playing—for one I look down and I never know when to use the "gas, the clutch, or the brake," lol, and this one is an automatic to boot. Now what? Haha. Then again—music has no rules, because it too, is art. I could be a pianist and not know it. Let's go with that.

Bye for now—

Love Mom

"As parents have a profound impact on their children, keep in mind these impacts aren't permanent. Changes can be made at any point along the journey. God is good at restoring broken things and renewing dysfunctional relationships." -Unknown

January 1st, 2020

Dear Riley;

I am out of the hospital, yay! It is incredibly hard to orchestrate your life from an institution. They confiscate your phone, if that paints a picture. And you only have access to it for a scheduled time frame in the morning. After a few newcomers to the ward, I stopped asking people what brought them there when it seemed I was on the suicide attempt ward. As relieved as I am, it is an experience I will never forget.

The first time I thought I miscarried you I was two months pregnant and got air lifted to a hospital in a bigger center. Once the ultrasound showed a heart the size of a clicker pen end and it was beating I knew I was still pregnant. I went downstairs to the gift shop and bought you a little rocking horse. It was the start of a collection of ornamental merry-go-round or rocking ponies. With all the moves and general carnage that is my life that assortment is long gone, but while I was in the hospital I made a little blue rocking horse and have now stuck it into your stash of childhood goods.

Then again at four months pregnancy I once again poured blood tested for an active pregnancy. I was also told there was "debris," inside of me next to you. What I believe now is that you were supposed to be a triplet, but you are the only survivor. Call me Fertile Mrytle.

When I found out I was six weeks pregnant I quit drinking, but I had drank while I didn't know so I told the doctor about it and they did all kinds of tests on you. You do not have affects of fetal alcohol syndrome whatsoever. But I thought you had the right to know everything pertaining to you.

I have always said; "I would rather be rejected for being authentic then be accepted for the games I play." But like the country song by Aaron Tippin; "I Wouldn't Have it Any Other Way," "there is a price for being me and that's what I'll have to pay," and Lord knows I have.

"Secrets are lies and bad manners besides." I don't know where that came from but I grew up with it.

Love, Mom

_____

_____

_____

"Don't let the errors of evil people lead you down the wrong path and make you lose your balance." II Peter 3:17 (CEV)

"Life is meant to be managed not cured." –Dr. Phil

January 2nd, 2020

Dear Riley;

I want you to know I forgive you for everything. While you were a child I was responsible for what went on; once you were an adult you were responsible for your actions and I forgive you for those.

How I wish you hadn't slipped through the cracks when you were suicidal in 2017. It is like they ignored you right in the emergency department. The nurse was such a...special piece of magic shall we say, asking me questions and then interrupting me to tell me I was giving the wrong answers. I wanted to give her a piece of my mind/nugget from my noggin but then I looked into the two black holes in her head that were her eyes and clamped my pie hole shut in a hurry. She was beyond burned out. The mind is just one more part of the body that can get overloaded and sick; also one more item that can be treated if not cured.

If you ever get diagnosed with a mental illness, you're still okay. God has lots of angels with clipped wings. They do groundwork, lol.

Your Dad was diagnosed with schizophrenia after a stint in solitary confinement. He was doing hard time in the "fed pen," for armed robbery of a convienience store. It was a seven year sentence all total. He didn't figure it had been a fair test at all.

When I met him he was the bad boy women swoon over; tall, dark, handsome, scarred, tattooed and mysterious. He wore glasses and was carrying books and his artwork... told me he was trying to turn his life around. I asked-nay, told him he was also about to help me move a hide-a-bed upstairs to my apartment so he obliged, lol.

Whenever I used to tell Rachel she IS going to do something she called it being "voluntold."

Random thought originally from your Aunt M2; "I don't suffer from insanity I quite enjoy it."

Haha. Love,

Mom

"If it falls apart that easily, there is nothing falling apart yet." –Grandma K

"Sometimes people get together even if it's in the devils's own wheelbarrow." Grandma and Grandpa K

January 3rd, 2020

Dear Riley;

After your Aboriginal Grandmother spent her time in residential school she stayed with the Roman Catholic faith like many other survivors. She also passed it on to her children so I am looking for a Rosary for you to remember your father by. It's one of those; "I will know it when I see it," type of situations.

Grandma F is such a rock. She has now buried four of her six children. How she keeps going is beyond me... let's just say I admire her strength.

When you were five the movie "Spirit," came out and you hounded me to get it. Your little voice was so cute.

When you were a toddler and you wanted more juice you would say; "moy? Moy?" And later it became: "some more juice happened?" Lol.

I wish I could hug you and stroke your hair for a while.

This past Christmas I got out all the ornaments you and Rachel ever made and put them on the tree. And then the cats decided they looked better on the floor so I packed them back up.

I pray "God deliver her of her hatred, anger, and bitterness." It will hurt you more than anyone else, maybe even literally.

Love, Mom

_____

_____

_____

"Be who you are, everyone else is taken."–Unknown

"Find out who you are and do it on purpose."–Dolly Parton

"No one can make you feel inferior without your consent."–Eleanor Roosevelt

January 4th, 2020

Dear Riley;

In my heart you will always be my little girl. Rachel too.

The art catastrophe in beadshop today is a clumsy keychain that reads: "I am the princess of crazy when you will play my song." Haha. Good cover.

The house I live in now is one you have not ever visited. It is such a kid house, with all kinds of nooks and a passageway even. You should come see it sometime. Or even better come back as a little kid to mess it up. How I miss that kind of messy house.

In middle school, you were bullied for being First Nations and one day you were so upset you came home and declared yourself oriental, lol. Then a caucasian boy from behind your seat picked on you and you told him to absolutely cut it out or you would slap the white right off him. There's nothing wrong with pointing out the facts or making promises of self defense.

On a random idea to google you I found a picture of you fancy dancing at a school you went to. Naturally a screen shot had to be taken...What a nice regalia.

In grade seven you went to four different schools. Wowsers. Have rebellion, will travel.

Little things have begun to matter more now that I am back in the regular world. Like the sound my winter boots make on the sidewalk while I walk Angelo. The hoarfrost on the tree branches. I wonder why it is called whorefrost, lol. Does that mean someone is charging for it? Ha ha.

You used to make the best Bannock. Probably still do.

Missing you more and liking it less...

Love, Mom

_____

_____

_____

"If you want to be happy, do not dwell in the past, do not worry about the future, focus on living fully in the present." -Roy T. Bennett

January 5th, 2020

Dear Riley;

The other day I was in the second hand store and saw buttons for sale at ten cents each. It reminded me of our button picture days and I wanted to buy them out. Maybe I will for memory's sake, that's what we all need right? More stuff and things. NOT.

This spring you will graduate with a Bachelor's Degree in Social Work, but I hope you get the help you need before you try and help anyone else. That is how it has to be, you put your own oxygen mask on first in the event of a crash, and man have you ever!

When you were eleven you randomly went to a friend's house after school without telling me and I had the police looking for you. I was passing ostriches. The same year you got your period and thought you were dying. What a year!

Your hair gel brand was called "Got2be," you specifically asked for it.

I miss your artwork. There is a stack of copies I made of three paintings but that is as far as I got in ever distributing them. Now they are all packed up for you, including the originals.

Once, I was exactly where you are, only I hated my father enough to wish him suffering or dead. So to be here in this place with you is not new, even though the reasons are different. Forgiveness does not change the story. But it makes one want to tell it less often. Hosea 8:7 says: "Those that sow wind shall reap a storm." (Paraphrase, mine). Amen to that. God set me free of the anger, bitterness, and rebellion and I know one day you will be free also.

Love and hugs,

Mom

_____

_____

_____

"In the process of gaining our rightful place, we must not be guilty of wrongful deeds. Let us not seek to satisfy our thirst for freedom by drinking from the cup of bitterness and hatred. We must forever conduct our struggle on the high plane of dignity and discipline."
Martin Luther King, Junior

January 6th, 2020

Dear Riley;

Even as a really little child you were obstinate, lol. When I wanted you to clean up your toys you refused so I would place my hands over top of yours and force the issue. We would end up on a giggling heap on the floor. If I said: "c'mon, eat your cereal we have to go somewhere," you would brush your bowl to the floor indignantly. I learned to give you straight plasticware; Corelle splinters when it breaks.

You hucked a finished bottle in the stroller into traffic if we were out walking. We lost alot of bottles to L Avenue in K because that's the path we took home from daycare.

When you went to Bible camp your picture made it into the brochure for the Bible camp that year; the back of you in a canoe. I sent it to your Dad without making a copy. Groaning out loud.

I remember you liked Keith Urban's song: "A Better Life." Well here's to hope and prayer for that.

Love Mom

"Never get mad at someone for being exactly who they are."–Unknown

"If we all knew exactly what the other person thought, none of us would be friends."–Unknown

January 7th, 2020

Dear Little Runningbird;

I used to call you that. It was an attempt to give you a First Nations name. When you got older you informed me that obtaining an aboriginal spiritual name had a certain rite of passage that involved elders, a sage smudge, and a ceremony, if I got that right.

We used to watch "Road To Avonlea," series in the basement suite when we didn't have cable. Right now its snowing and blowing outside and it reminded me of the show, they had some nasty winter scenes. So did Little House on the Prairie but we didn't get into that as much.

Remember, I'm not sending you all your childhood stuff through your grandparents to disown you, I am sending it because you wanted it.

If I could paint portraits I would paint yours. A big canvas of your second year graduation from the social work program.

I pray the word of God over you; "Give us now as much happiness as the sadness you gave us during all our years of misery. Let us, your servants, see your mighty deeds; let our descendants see your glorious might. Lord our God, may your blessings be with us. Give us success in all we do!" Psalms 90:15-17. (GNB) Amen.

When I look back at how poor we were while I raised you I wonder why I didn't give you and Rachel to someone who could actually afford to raise children?! It was selfish, I realize now; but who exists because we are affordable? Haha. I don't.

One thing I appreciate about poverty is that it forces you into your creative zone. I have bought used brand name items or no name brand new, depending what it was. When you and Rachel reached pre-teen years; "Tweenagers," I called you; we were all soooo sick of second hand we decided no more used footwear. Shoes conform to the shape of each individual foot so it was a good call. Now I will still buy a pair of used pumps if I am only going to be in them for an hour at church or something.

Remember to be yourself—everyone else is taken. Lol.

Love Mom

_____

_____

_____

"I choose to live by choice, not by chances; to be motivated, not manipulated; to make changes, not excuses."–Unknown

"You are either building your dreams or someone elses."–Unknown

January 8th, 2020

Dear Riley;

I pray God does whatever it takes to get you back into the kingdom of light. You are a King's kid.

Do you remember when I called you: "the papoose from Bruce?" You even signed some of your cards to me that way.

You were such a junk food junkie, especially sweet stuff. I fed you fruits and vegatables and your sweet tooth developed first. Just like the public health nurse said.

Everything went wrong with the pregnancy that was you. And for the longest time I blamed myself for my fornicative lifestyle, as if married people have no trouble with conception. I had a miscarriage at two and four months of the same pregnancy and the technicians said "there is debris trapped next to the baby." One day for the sake of your own healing you will have to grieve the loss of your siblings.

In a session in the psychward, talking about the first miscarriage and the messy second pregnancy, I told the doctor; "I think I suffer from complicated grief syndrome," and just like that, something lifted off of me and I knew right there if I had been I no longer did.

I wonder how many people were one of two or more babies per pregnancy and are messed up because of it. Your subconscious knows. A guy I knew —a chronic womanizer; kept saying "she's just like a sister to me..." And I wondered if that was what it was all about. Searching for the lost sibling. Someone told me that once you grieve the loss you are okay.

Anyway, the verse in Isaiah 49:17 (NKJV) "Your sons hasten back; your destroyers and those who laid you waste shall go away from you," has taken on a new meaning to me. It haunted me. I finally asked God what it was about. And it is how God confirmed I have more than one son in heaven; "there are others,"he said. I asked "what are their names?" "You tell me," he says. Bailey-Jean (my first pregnancy) I knew, but it was 25 years since I lost him and my complaint with God had been: "I never got to see his face." Then because God honors me, he showed me a kid in the hospital who resembled my oldest son. "See?" He said; "He is one of mine but he also looks like one of yours. I still save two of everything."You should have seen him change while I prayed for him, he came out of his shell, he walked a straight line, laughed a mirthful laugh and even started holding conversations which had been impossible when he first arrived. The God let me name Denver Carlyle, and Miles Emile, the other two babies in with you. They are tall dark and handsome and they look like their older brother Bailey-Jean because of how good God is. He honored me as a mother, nothing more nothing less. Religious pharisees like to point fingers and judge obvious sins that happen to be different than theirs. Isaiah 43:4 says; "Since you are precious and honored in my sight, and because I love you, I will give people in exchange for you, nations in exchange for your life." (NIV).

Remember how I used to tell you girls that in our family there are no halves and no steps. God had to kill his perfect son to make us eligible for adoption and then His legitimate children, so surely we can imitate Him and adopt people as full family members.

It wasn't really helpful that you were born struggling to breathe, whisked away from me for those crucial first four hours after your birth. Maybe you think I am making excuses, but I am giving you all the pieces of your life I possibly can.

Since the hospital stay, I have decided to experience not suffer, and it makes all the difference. It gets you out of victim mode. After all a victim is just a: Very Insecure Child Trapped In Muck.

Love, Mom

_____

_____

_____

"You keep track of all my sorrows. You have collected all my tears in your bottle. You have recorded each one in your book." Psalm 56:8(NLT).

January 9th, 2020

Dear Riley;

Everything you ever needed to know about men you learned in first grade: boys are yucky. Haha. I once saw a coffee mug that read: "when God created men she was only joking." Oh can't you just hear the religious tongues clucking now. I think He can handle a joke, He is not fragile.

You're just like the girl in the book I named you after, you have a good connection to your Grandpa. He would do anything for you, he is not the same guy today who raised me.

A tooth and two locks of hair are no longer in your collection of childhood memorabilia. I had a funeral to help myself grieve your loss so they went into the earth. I stroked the hair one more time, so velvety soft, like putting your fingers in cornstarch. And then I realized too late Aboriginals either burn loose hair or release them in water. Duh.

In your younger years in school, we suspected one of your teachers took a piece of your artwork home and never gave it back.

Your dad and I used to watch a sitcom called: "Family Matters," and laugh at Steve Erkle and his use of the word: "perturbed" a lot. It seems aboriginals love to giggle and have fun—you can hardly stop once you start laughing.

I hope your pop made it to heaven. God forgives—people make lists. I chose to forgive a man who once tried to spit on me. We should all forgive as much as we hope to receive mercy, grace and forgiveness.

Love, Mom

_____

_____

_____

"There is no greater agony than bearing an untold story inside you." —Maya Angelou (deceased)

"Don't wait for the light at the end of the tunnel, stride down there and light the bloody thing yourself."—Unknown

January 10th, 2020

Dear Riley;

There was this one day when we were out with the double stroller and we found a kite half buried in the dusty gutter. I picked it up, washed it off and we went back and flew it while Rachel slept in the buggy. You and I had so much fun. You were just over two years old...it was a beautiful spring day with just enough breeze to catch the kite as I held it over my head and ran down the hill on F Road to start it. It was such a good day.

The other day I took your pictures out and put them up along with our family photos. In the stash I found some of your drawings and the feeling like someone kidnapped you and only left these behind as a ransom note, only there was no where to go or phonecall to answer so I cried out to God. I know Big Daddy hears me.

On your third birthday my camara broke and it was a good thing I had a picture of you very close to the date. Phew. We had a little picnic party on the patio of our ground floor apartment, just you and I while Rachel snoozed.

Then on your grade ninth graduation I dropped your camara and broke it...your mother is a gazelle did I mention?

Those were the days my volunteer job in a local church basement provided food and clothing for us; even the odd bauble or two.

Love, Mom

_____

_____

_____

"Life is never so hard that it is impossible to live, nor so difficult that it is easy to live." –Unknown

"You have within you, right now, everything you need to deal with whatever the world can throw at you." –Unknown

"At the end of the day we can endure much more than we think we can." –Frida Kahlo

January 17th, 2020

Dear Riley;

It cracks me up that you are so much like me and there's nothing you can do about it. Hee hee.

Many prayers go up for reconciliation of my little family that you are part of. One day we will all be together again.

If I was ever given an aboriginal name it would be Many Prayers.

You were raised so poor we hardly ever had sheets on the bed. Then when things got better I had a hard time convincing you and your sister that people didn't just sleep on straight mattresses. You were used to bedding being torn up to be utilized as coffee filters and toilet paper.

There were many miracles too, like one Easter I found two collectible dolls at the dump still in their boxes just in time for gifts for you and Rachel at the end of a treasure hunt.

We made juice out of jello powder before it gelled and I made homemade playdoh. We were poor yet there was always provision, you know?

You were not into dolls much though, when you were a toddler I heard an "Aaaaak! I broke my dolly's leg, I broke my dolly's leg!" So I went flying to see what was the matter and there you were with a doll in two pieces. I popped the leg back in but things were not the same for you after that around dolls. I wonder if there is any connection to that and your experience in the womb beside two others.

It's incredibly hard not to be able to love who you love. Love is a hard habit to break and maybe I do not ever want to be cured.

Well I have to go walk the dog. Actually I think he walks me and I appreciate his efforts.

Love, Mom

"Difficult roads often lead to beautiful destinations."–Unknown

"Faith makes no provision for failure."–Unknown

"Failure is success in progress."–Unknown

January 12th, 2020

Dear Riley;

I can visit you every time I open this book. It's kinda cool.

Hopefully and prayerfully you get the help you need for good mental health before you try and help everybody else. You're a very giving person. Always were. We shouldn't take from ourselves though, there are enough people who would suck us dry if allowed.

When we lived on F Avenue in K____, you were three years old and went through a phase where you peed on the floor and kept on playing. You were potty trained but the bathroom and all its formalities were too far away and too much of a process. Lol.

This summer on July 4th is your K grandparents 50th wedding aniversary. Not that any wedded bliss was involved. We are simply giving them credit for time served. Haha.

Your Grandfather was sure proud of the drum you made for him. It hangs on the wall in his office. He even tries playing it sometimes. Enough said.

We sure moved around alot when you were young. Our record time spent in a place was three years. Gypsies, we were. I still never see a road I don't want to go down.

Gotta run,

Love, Mom

_____

_____

_____

"Women are angels

And when someone breaks our wings

We simply continue to fly

On a broomstick.

We are flexible like that."–Unknown

January 13th, 2020

Dear Riley;

You have inherited my insomnia. Did you ever sleep? Haha. As a small baby you did.

Rachel told me you bought a pink car. Just like the makeup Mindy doll you had to have when you were four. Your step father searched high and low for it until he found one for you. (Rachel's Dad) He wasn't all bad.

We are all a mixture of good and evil, with a beast in the basement and an angel in the attic, it matters who we feed the most. And the one that controls us the most is the one we have fed the best.

Repetition is the language of trauma, I read somewhere. So is forgetfulness. Often I remember something about you and before I get a chance to write it down; poof! It's gone. Arrgh.

You will hopefully visit this quaint annoying little town I live in one day, so full of old buildings and farming history. So historically beautiful.

When you were a baby you resembled your sister N—from another mother when she was a baby. Say that five times backwards haha.

When we lived right on the lake you, your sister and I used to pile into my bed and watch Grace Under Fire and The Simpsons.

Miss you,

Love, Mom

_____

_____

_____

"Why fit in when you were born to stand out?" -Dr. Suess

"To fall in love with yourself is the first secret to happiness."-Robert Morley

"You need to give yourself permission to be human."-Joyce Brothers

January, 14th 2020

Dear Riley;

It's so cold outside right now all the lawyers and politicians have their hands in their own pockets and teenagers are finally pulling their jeans up over their asses.

I was glad when I found out there was funding for you through my disability pension. It might not make up for all the years I raised you in poverty, but it is something anyway. How I detest the word disability, but don't we all have things we cannot do.

Your dad and I liked going for walks in the rain holding hands. Rain water is good for your hair, although there was nothing good enough to fix the awful haircut he had given himself other then three weeks. The difference between a good and a bad haircut is usually about three weeks, did you know.

He wore a bandana like a biker over his head alot so I taught him the german word "dueck," because mennonite women wear them on their heads too, only they don't tuck in the point. Bruce was soooo handsome. That's why you are here, lol. Priorities, man.

God told me he can only really use your passion for his purposes and I believe it.

"But now this is what the Lord says: 'Do not weep any longer, for I will reward you,' says the Lord. "Your children will come back to you from the distant land of the enemy." Jeremiah 31:16 (NLT)

Amen to that.

Love, Mom

_____

_____

_____

"Jerusalem, I can never forget you! I have written your name on the palms of my hands." Isaiah 49:16 (NIV).

January 15th, 2020

Dear Riley:

God has a tattoo of you and He thinks you are to die for.

When you were still a "babe in arms," you went through a phase of calling every male we ran into "daddy." It was the days before the internet superhighway and I could not find your "fotah," (father) for anything. And ofcourse with your step dad out of our lives you went without a literal father figure for so many years but God is your Father. Always was always will be. In His family there are no halves nor steps either.

You were eleven when you finally talked to him on the phone for the first time, and that's how your relationship stayed for the next three years. He'd had a real bad accident–is there such a thing as a good one?! And he was talking about it constantly. It almost took his life.

People call pregnancies "accidents," and I cringe. There are no accidental human beings.

Your Dad had a heavy french accent for someone who didn't speak it and was so far removed down the line of King Louie. He said things like; "I can respig thet,"

(I can respect that) and such and such; "annehways."
My personal favourite; "fug thet." Lol.

Both your Dad and I had and have a dry sense of
humor so you are stuck with one also.

On one of your earlier life pictures we are sitting on
the couch, you in just a diaper, a "plumpkin" and I am
wearing a shirt that says: "sometimes when I stop and
think I forget to get started again." Lol.

Talk at you tomorrow,

Love, Mom

"What luck for leaders that men men don't think."-
Adolf Hitler

"Evil triumphs when good men do nothing."-Edmund
Burke

January 16th, 2020

Dear Riley;

I packed a before and after picture of a lamp I rebuilt
for you. The original base had broken so I stuck the
bulb and the long bolt it sat on into the opening of
a whiskey jug and painted it, then plastered it with
little decorations, fridge magnets, hair clips and
curlers...all items to do with a little girls life.

At the time we lived on 725 F Avenue in K-----,
B.C., but it is probably commercialized by now. It
was a strip of post war houses and our back yard at
"Joyful"Avenue, (F---- translated) was amazing, it
stretched on forever and it was fenced with a garden
plot.

We never lived anywhere for long, our record has been 2
years at B--- Road and three years at the apartment
in downtown R--- but you were not there the entire
time.

It would have been hard to raise two happy, well
adjusted children without being single, brokefolk
as broke as a joke and having a case of C.P.T.S.D. from

years and incidents and trauma. I have changed the meaning of the words to: Christ's Promises Transforming to Sustaining Deliverance.

The Bible says our labor isn't in vain in the Lord; 1st Corinthians 15:58. Hallelujah for that! Hopefully as mothers can take that literally. Haha.

I am getting better at walking on a broken heart; better at life without you. The way we were wasn't working anyway. We butted heads since you were born, practically.

Love, Mom

_____

_____

_____

"If suffering perfects the soul, someone is trying to make a saint out of me!" (Good luck with that) – Unknown

"I choose not to suffer, I choose to experience." – Me.

January 17th, 2020

Dear Riley;

If grandchildren are a grandparents revenge, I can't wait. Tee hee.

Today when I googled you I found a youtube vidoe of you wearing glasses talking about "Jordan's Principle." Your granny Fontaine had a video up of her talking to an interviewer about her beadwork but now I can't find it. Annehways, you looked really good.

Do you remember the F---- Park where we spent so much time? It has since morphed into an apartment complex. For a while we kept a rock from there but it stayed in the lake place in the flower bed of the trailer, number 4-1935 B--- Road, I think.

Some day, hopefully while the skill is still out there, I want to have all the negatives of photos I have converted to disc. Or if I could find an app that actually works to scan a negative and produce as a picture.

When we first moved to R--- I took you girls to the library alot. We walked because we had no car, and once we bought groceries for a picnic and by the time we purchased each individual's wants it was a forty some dollar deal, but whatever—we carried them to the city hall park and ate there. It was so pretty and peaceful...for a town labeled as the 5th most dangerous place in Canada to live. Another time we bought pizza from the store downtown and walked around the corner and sat on the Presbyterian Church steps to eat it. Talk about a "topping," haha.

Love, Mom

"The only job where you start at the top is digging a hole." -unknown

"If you are not living on the edge you are taking up too much space." -unknown

"Opportunity only knocks once. After that it's the neighbor wanting to borrow the snowblower." -unknown

January 18th, 2020

Dear Riley;

When we lived in R--- of K-----, and we always lived in that part of town, the poor side of the tracks; we built a snowman and snow woman and dressed them right up. Then someone stole the hats, scarves, and gloves right off the couple. I guess they needed them more.

On that particular street, close to Highway 33, we happened to look outside one day and see the house across the street catch fire while we ate supper. It turned out to be a grow operation that ignited while the occupants were not home. They lied to Grandma T at the church community services; "we were all sitting down at teh table having supper when a fire started in the little boys bedroom..." Uh huh. That's why the firemen had to kick down the front door and all the lights were out when we watched it start... most people seem to have something to hide and I agree secrets are to sickness as openness is to wholeness. Even pillars in the community are sometimes just piles of baloney. Lol.

Growing up poor seems to be a disease that gets passed on from generation to generation. So does wealth. One of my prayers is that you and Rachel get out of that—heck I am still trying.

Many prayers and much love,

Mom

_____

_____

_____

"I will lead the blind by ways they have not known, along unfamiliar paths I will guide them; I will turn darkness into light before them and make the rough places smooth. These are the things I will do; I will not forsake them." Isaiah 42:16 (NIV).

January 19th, 2020

Dear Riley;

There's a story of a woman whose mother had Alzheimer's. She said she watched her mother deplete from her original personality until there was only ten percent left of the original woman, and that last ten percent was still a hundred percent her Mom, came the resolution.

Maybe you could find a percentage of motherliness that you could still work with in me.

I know how much you hate your one cousin, but hatred not only makes you a murderer by Biblical standards it is not freeing. I like it better when I just don't anything some people, although nowhere in the book have I ever found listed that apathy is a godly virtue.

Love is a hard habit to break and it is hard not to be allowed to love whom you love. If God didn't carry me I would be a puddle on the floor.

It is comforting to know God has the same kind of kids we do; rebellious, cruel, ungrateful, betraying, abandoning and so on. There is nothing He hasn't seen already and experienced long before the event even happened.

You said you were putting a curse on me in one of those emails, and I remembered how Jesus allowed himself to made into a curse and hung on the cross to nullify every other curse. The Bible says in 2nd Timothy 4:18 (NASB) that "the Lord will rescue me from every evil deed and bring me safely into His heavenly Kingdom. To Him be the glory forever and ever! Amen.

"No one can deliver out of my hand. When I act, who can reverse it?" Isaiah 43:13 (NIV).

I talked to God about the spiritism you are into and He said it is no problem, you have to be educated in order to speak against it one day. He said you are in training for His glory and purpose. Wow. That sure beats the feeling that my babies have been kidnaped in a dark suv and driven off the cliff without a number to call. That's how hopeless I have felt about you and Rachel turning against God, but He assures me I don't need 9-1-1 when I can call on Him about this.

Love, Mom

_____

_____

_____

"An arrow can only be shot by pulling it backwards. So, when life is dragging you back, it means that it's going to launch you into something great."—Unknown

January 20, 2020

Dear Riley;

Hey Tweedlebug. That was one nickname I gave you, one of many.

Do you remember the story I used to tell you of how God made the different races? He was baking cookies and one batch turned out dark, the next round turned out pale...so far we have black and caucasians...the third batch was neither black nor white but a golden brown and they were the aboriginals. It is just an allegory... but these days most people are soooooo offended over sooo little, and I say: "Taking offense when there is none being given is theft."

We are all God's children by creation, then when we believe in Jesus His Son, we become God's children again spiritually. Hence we are all from the same Father.

Love, Mom

_____

_____

_____

"There is no life without a task; no person without a talent; no place without a fragment of God's light waiting to be discovered and redeemed; no situation without its possibility of sanctification; no moment without its call." –Jonathan Sacks

January 27th, 2020

Dear Riley;

I've been losing children since I could make them. When I lost your older brother who was aboriginal also, I never got to see his face and I thought must be the worst penalty. It prepared me for losing you and I have seen your face.

You were right about not being my kid. You belong to God our creator.

Through the grapevine I heard your engagement broke off. Hopefully that was a good thing. Sometimes things fall apart so better things can fall together. Marilyn Monroe said that.

You look so much like Pochahontas. You're the action figure, lol.

The house I live in is directly behind a cemetary. I tell everyone my neighbors are quiet, haha. Do you remember when I took you and Rachel to a graveyard in the lake and we read the headstones to try to decipher the story of the people buried there?

Anyway, sometimes it's good to remind oneself that life is good, it always beats a tombstone.

I live next to Janette Oake's nephew. He is a confirmed "bachelor 'til the rapture," and the nephew of one of my favourite authors. Once in a while I play a prank on him. Once I made him a to-do list on a roll of adding machine paper and on the last line I said there could be more...and pictured him unfurling the thing until the end and finding nothing. But it blew off his vehicle as he was driving since he had no seen it earlier. Harump.

I am publishing a trilogy. Woot woot. Let's hope it goes bestseller. See, ya don't have to have all that fancy book learnin' to make something of your life. You don't even have to write a book...you give your life to Christ and let Him worry about what purpose it will have.

You are probably art-and-crafting your way through university for extra money.

Trying to hard to recall details about you can cause me to draw a blank, so I will just let the memories come to me. Grief and trauma do things to you, but I choose not to suffer, I choose to experience...Beauty from ashes...always.

Love, Mom

"You may not control all the events that happen to you, but you can decide not to be reduced by them."
—Maya Angelou (deceased).

January 22, 2020

Dear Riley;

Please do yourself a favor and lose my married last name. We owe that name zero homage after how it turned out and the way he was. And my research tells me the last name comes from the male side of the family.

Joke: how many kids with ADHD does it take to screw in a light bulb?

Answer: wanna go for a bike ride? Haha.

That alphabetical disorder runs in the family tree big time.

Your favourite place to live was the trailer on the lake. The highway was behind and above us, the lake in front of and below us. The mobile home was patched together like a jigsaw puzzle. Like your grandmother's house on D Street.

You must be glad to be out of R————. What a cantankerous slaughterhouse. A ballistic town. It's where our little family truly fell apart, but I have hope and many prayers for healing and reconciliation.

You have a lot of amends to make, even if other people were wrong also. Conflict is never one sided, but there is power in washing our side of the window clean and expecting nothing in return except having done the right thing.

Love, Mom

_____

_____

_____

"If you want happiness for an hour, take a nap. If you want happiness for a day, go fishing. If you want happiness for a year, inherit a fortune. If you want happiness for a lifetime, help someone else." –Chinese Proverb

January 23rd, 2020

Dear Riley;

December 15th, 2019th was going to be the day of my passing. I wasn't going to tell you about this but it isn't like our relationship has anywhere to go but up.

After some radical facebook slander from what I suspect was a connection to the shady security company I helped shut down and your immense addiction to your hatred and bitterness of me spelled out in blood curdling emails...the judgemental church group I was attending...I had had it. Oh– I like to think I can take a pretty good ass whooping before I lay down and holler 'nuff; but forty plus years of someone's foot on my neck I had enough. What is incredibly hard to take is the snobs that contributed to my personal pain looking down their nose yet again for my breakdown. This is a redneck town, "it ain't cool to have mental health issues." Don't they know delusions of grandeur are counted as such?!

It was noon when I started chugging the hard stuff from under the Christmas tree meant for someone else.

Thirty-five percent alcohol and I am not a big person. I made a phonecall to a friend who only loves the sound of his own voice and he was no help whatsoever but in all fairness my mind was made up. Whoever said God looks after babies and drunks wasn't kidding. Actually I think it is a verse in the Bible. Your grandmother K was in a housefire before I was born and suffered severe burns from the hip to the lip in all degrees. I survived.

By the time I finished the useless phonecall and held the sleeping pills to my lips I passed out and tipped the pill bottle to the floor as I passed out and hit the kitchen counter on the way down.

When the doorbell woke me up hours had passed—it was now about suppertime and either I had made it to my bed or the dog had dragged me there. A cop was standing outside and he said Rachel had worried when all contact had dropped off from me. I caught sight of my hideous reflection in the door window and saw a Lisa Simpson on meth with blonde hair sticking up everywhere and black makeup running all over her face.

He came in—he went into the kitchen and at some point must have had to reef me to my feet because besides the egg on my head I had bruises on my forearms like grab marks. Memory of that day still cuts in and out like reading a book with every other page torn out.

The officer, according to his paperwork took one look at the pill spill all over the counter and read the bottle then said; "ok we are going to the hospital." I didn't argue. I put my coat on, walked dumbly out to the police truck in my slippers and tried to get into the front seat. He drove me to the hospital and when the staff stuck a needle in my arm to start an intravenous fluid flush my blood ran like water. There was some medical jargon flying around the room then, roughly translated: "Oh crap, she is not coagulating." Then I did but they had to change the sheets.

Anyway, they pumped fluids and by morning I was a happy drunk and didn't feel like dying anymore, but they sectioned me and sent me to Ponoka. That means I was no longer a free person until I was assessed by mental health professionals. Section 10," the act is called when they do that.

I recovered quickly from what I now believe was a complete nervous breakdown and only spent two weeks in hospital with a lot of passes.

The victim stance is the worst. It means you are not in control, that people do things to you and life happens to you.

One day I pray you will let me be part of your healing. My parents still sometimes hurt me because of the way they are sometimes and I hope that will not be the case with us. They would not visit me in the hospital but admitted they would have come to the funeral. Weird.

I felt I had to reach down deep inside myself to find love for you after the way it's been for the last few years. Volatile. However I want to give as much grace, mercy and forgiveness as I need to receive and it is probably a Jesus-sized amount.

See, in pesty adulthood and graduation from victimhood, one has to own what they bring to the table in a relationship. We all need to take our own inventory, not each others.

For you, I wish a healthy romantic relationship one day also. Not like what you have had, I am thinking.

Alberta has a high rate of domestic violence and it seems to pool in Central Region. I think a cop told me that. I have even experienced emotional and psychological abuse in so-called friendship.

One of the things I have kicked myself for is moving us to this province, but I am from here. It is counter-productive to beat yourself up - more domestic abuse, technically. Haha.

Love, Mom

_____

_____

_____

"Sometimes the best you can do is not think, not wonder, not obsess. Just breathe and have faith that everything will turn out for the best." -Unknown

January 24th, 2020

Hello Tweedle;

I used to have answers now I have kids. Wish I could hold you and stroke your long hair. You used to fall asleep when I stroked your left eyebrow.

Your first word was your name; "Eye-lee." You said it in your swing where you napped three times a day. Too many some might say but you grew up to hold down three jobs at times so...eerie coincidence I guess.

We were dirt poor and lived off of food banks, charities and churches. Sometimes I think poverty creates a mental illness because it makes life so brutally hard it almost cuts you in half. Still, I always gave what I could where I could in time or recycled products I couldn't use.

Your favourite show was at one time "Franklyn," and you would pretend to be the turtle when you played. "I'm Frank-koo-lyn," you would say. Cute.

Today was one of those days where you'd get a paper cut from a get well card. Everything slipped away at least once. Haha.

It is getting a little bit more doable with the grief of losing you. For the longest time I felt like I was at a funeral where the lid never got closed. But life goes on no matter what.

Or this is simply an easier day— I will acept that as a gift.

Love, Mom

P.S. The quote today is totally for you, my anxious child.

_____

_____

_____

"You intended to harm me, but God intended it for good to accomplish what is now being done, the saving of many lives." Genesis 50:20 (NIV).

January 25th, 2020

Dear Riley;

You are on your way back to God. Hell hath no chance against a mother's faith. He has never left you nor forsaken you even though you walked away take it from someone who knows. This rebellion is a generational thing.

It's so peaceful here, you would love the yard around my house, complete with firepit. Correction— fire rim.

Last summer I planted a perennial that looked like an Indian Paintbrush plant in my flower bed. since it reminded me of you.

When you were little I had a hard time convincing people your artwork was yours because you were so precocious.

Would you believe your sister is finally interested in learning how to cook. Some years ago you and I were going to force her into a foods class if nothing else.

You were born a scientist, filling and dumping cups of water and various household products, lol.

Do you remember the stickbug you brought home from summer camp and I accidentally killed because I thought the poor thing looked cold and gave it a light bulb for its aquarium. They actually reproduce by breaking a piece off of themselve that continues on...a literal chip off the block, lol. It can only produce female offspring that way, though, not males.

Love, Mom

_____

_____

_____

"There will be obstacles. There will be doubters. There will be mistakes. But with hard work, there are no limits." –Unknown

"Our fatigue is often caused not by work, but by worry, frustration, and resentment." –Dale Carnegie

January 26th, 2020

Dear Riley;

It is sometimes hard to pull up a recent memory of your hatred and venom and write to you as if you will ever be receptive again.

I forgive you for what I perceive to be toxic, cruel disrespect of me but I will not ever allow it to pipe my way again. My human rights haven't dried up yet and they never will. I won't ever need a connection to anyone so badly that I will allow myself to be abused.

At the point of true adulthood, we realize we have to own our stuff and I don't think you have yet. In that revelation also comes the dawning that our parents are mere human beings whose hearts can be broken also. My own words–my own experiences.

Reaping and sowing is no respector of persons. The Bible says; "those that sow wind shall reap a storm." Your turn is coming, and when it does, it will be a doosie. Will I then be expected to fix it for you? Would you have the gall to even expect it? Demand it even?!

Well it won't happen. I will love you enough to let you fall and fully experience the pain and consequences of your actions. No matter what that looks like. It's something I should have done a long time ago.

Today the anger over how our relationship turned out is back, and how the connection has become such a dark spot in my life.

It is hard not to lapse back into victim mode and I am fighting it by not putting too much emphasis on feelings. They are neither right or wrong, they just are. I mean— trapped gas is a feeling and feelings change with what you eat.

God help me to keep loving you, to love myself, and forgive both of us— two human sinners headed straight for grace, mercy and the restoration thereof.

And thank you, Big Daddy (God) for the beauty that is coming out of this pile of ashes.

Amen. And with love, Mom

_____

_____

_____

"Instead of worrying about what you canot control, shift your energy to what you can create." -Roy T. Bennet

January 27th, 2020

Dear Riley;

Having an addictive personality and being someone experiencing the long term effects of post trauma I loved you to death and at times couldn't love you at all, thanks so myself. It is my firm philosophy that having the abilty to get addicted is not all negative; it is what enables us to stick out a relationship or a job and a stable life.

I will tell you things about me not as a narcissist like you labeled me, but AS YOUR MOTHER WHOM YOU ARE PART OF AND FROM. Suck it up princess. I am your mother and there isn't a flaming thing you can do about it. Hee hee. I am kind of enjoying aspects of it and regretting other parts of it.

You seem to have inherited my voice and my once upon a time victim mentality. I still hear it sometimes when I speak but change takes time. It's either woe is me or wow is God ever going to transform this situation. I can hardly wait. If there is no change there is no change there is no change and stuff be changing girl.

The quote for today is so true...instead of ruminating oneself to death over some unresolved conflict or issue like human nature tends to lean toward, getting into a craft of hobby gives one back some power. It's probably why you and Rachel did so many crafts in the; "kids who witness abuse program," and possibly why they have so many crafts and creative activities in the psych ward. It gives you back so much. I could be a ceramics junkie. Lol.

You used to say "I'm a crafty kid."

Love; Mom

_____

_____

_____

"Ships don't sink because of the water around them; ships sink because of the water that gets in them. Don't let what is happening around you get inside you and weigh you down."

January 28th, 2020

Dear Riley;

When you were three and we lived on F———— Avenue with the phenomenal back yard, you and I made snow angels in the back. I said; "Ok now stay there so you can help Mommy stand up again." I only needed the teensiest tug for momentum but instead you ran away giggling. So when it was your turn to make a snow person, I pretended you were bread dough and squished you further into the snow, giggle giggle, haha. Fun!

On the picture of you dancing as a fancy dancer, it looks like you found use for the mukluks I gave you. Or the calf part of them anyway. The foot section was way too small.

You used to love eating cheese. I wish you were here now so we could tear into a giant wheel from the grocery store...but that probably sounds cheesey. Haha.

Gotta go. Love, Mom

_____

_____

_____

"Better a live dog than a dead lion." -Doug Batchelor

"To conquer another you must first conquer yourself."-Plato

"Don't believe everything you think."-Unknown

January 29th, 2020

Dear Riley;

You and Rachel used to drape yourselves all over each other and call each other pricks, lol. Now our little family is split three ways and there is only three of us to begin with.

These days I pray against grandchildren, having lived the life of unplanned pregnancies and fornication. People judge, God forgives, consequences stay. I pray for you girls to have children under the right circumstances. Or perhaps not at all, depending on God's will. This world isn't exactly getting easier to live in and I cannot just be gaga over the thought of having cute little grandkids to cuddle. This is not about me.

I can't remember when the teenage rebellion started with you it seems it was always that way. Well? Forgiveness has zippety to do with slipping into an upright coma and lapsing into an unreality. Nope.

Sometimes I can picture you in jail easier than anywhere else. (Forgive me Lord for my unbelief). And if you end up in jail, I would visit if you were civil. If you wanted me to. If not, my life steadily goes on without you.

Oh, how I pray for you to be delivered of evil.

Love, Mom

_____

_____

_____

"For he is our peace, who made both groups one and tore down the dividing wall of hostility. Ephesians 2:14 (GSB).

January 30th, 2020

Dear Riley;

I have revised the serenity prayer for myself: God, grant me the serenity and ABILITY to accept that I can't change anybody else, give me the courage to acknowledge what needs changing about me and the wisdom to know that I can only grow and transform with your grace, mercy, love and forgiveness. Help me always to be willing to impart the tonnes of grace I know I also need to receive. Amen.

Meh. It might get revised again. You had written the orignial serenity prayer on one of your drawings.

There are two complete bedrooms upstairs here, I had to cut a box spring in half, fold it like a book, clamp it, and drag it upstairs so it would fit the narrow halls and stairwells of this remodeled old hotel. A rooming house, it was called. Total strangers shared a bathroom here with about a half dozen others and now I can't get a roommate because there is not a second bathroom.

Times have changed.

It is amazing what you can do when you have to. Live without your child, live alone except with the herd of animals I am usually surrounded by.

The landlord said there is a ghost here, a lady who used to own and run the hotel. She refers to her as; "the little b--- upstairs." She even described her as a small woman wearing button up booties like Laura Ingalls, a lot of red lipstick, necklaces that covered her throat, a yellow skirt and a blue blouse. Once in a while you heard stomping upstairs in quick little jabs. I have woke up to a tight hand on my throat and went to push whoever away and realized it was a spiritual problem. So when I could breathe again I told her to get out in Jesus name. I have done that several times, then asked that seven good hosts or spirits be brought in to replace the bad one otherwise the evil spirit leaves and returns with all their buddies and it gets worse. She is gone now. Phewff.

We definetley live in an interlocking realm with what we physically see and what we see emotionally and spiritually. It's a fascinating phenomenon.

Love, Mom

_____

_____

_____

"Human kindness has never weakened the stamina of softened the fibre of free people. A nation does not have to be cruel to be tough." -Franklin D. Roosevelt

January 31st, 2020

Dear Riley;

There is a framed picture on my wall with two little children sitting on a rock together, one is holding a book and one is fishing. A blonde and a redhead. I pried open the professional framework and colored the little redhead's hair black. Now it is a painting of my two little girls...at a glance.

I've been having more children since my hysterectomy thanks to having driven a schoolbus and teaching Sabbath and Sunday school. It's great. Oh- I have to give them back, but they are so sweet. It reminds me of the Bible verse; "Sing, O barren woman, you who never bore a child; burst into song, shout for joy, you who were never in labor; because more are the children of the desolate woman than of her who has a husband," says the Lord." Isaiah 54:1(NIV). I am living proof.

You have talked as if I never did anything right as a parent. It all depends on the perception you want to feed. I know I didn't turn out to be the parent I set out to be- who does? I used to have answers now I have kids. And before I ever had "chillins" I could have got up and taught a parenting class. Not now.

I remember crawling under chain link fencing to get to the pop bottles on the other side— that and to give the chicken the day off, haha.— so we could turn them in for money towards your New York Trip. I pawned my accordians so we could make the payments. I went without root canals that I needed so you and Rachel could have music lesson that you wanted. I slept on the living room floors of two bedroom apartments so that you could each have your own bedroom...I did some things right.

I wish things had been more stable; less moving, less abusive boyfriends, less mood swings and depression. I regret you and Rachel didn't know what you were coming home to, she complained everytime she went away on a sleepover for a weekend when she came back a certain someone had weasled his way back into our lives becuase after all; "this time would be different," with all the same behaviours.

No one has the power to change the past except —God— and He won't, so there is some feast for thought. All I can do is stand in my power and acknowledge what I regret and am sorry for, forgive myself even if no one else does, and move on.

You and Rachel are and were always enough. Don't let my mistakes lie to you.

Anything can be healed with God, guts, and grace. He does not force anyone's will though. That's why there is so much unresolved conflict in this world I am sure.

One day kid. One day.

Love, Mom

_____

_____

_____

"There is a difference between solitude and isolation. One is connected and one isn't. Solitude replenishes, isolation diminishes." -Henry Cloud

February 1st, 2020

Dear Riley;

You used to stand on your bike and break into the dining room window even though the front door was unlocked. I am not sure what that was about. Skill building for a resume? Lol.

I have moved to H, did I tell you, a small town of about 3000 people, and a typical small town it is. A conversation equals commitment and presents are promises, a question means complete interest in another not just some. People just ASSume until its a sea of asses and I am tired of being judged.

Still, isn't R----- a good place to be from?! It is the brown spot on the map of Alberta, haha. Your Dad gave me whatfor for moving there. Man, he was generous with giving heck, lol. Always full of advice for everyone else. Such a good looker too. For most of his life. I don't know what he looked like in the end.

Maybe one day you will tell me what he died of. At age 54 too, wow. He never even made the low end of seniorhood; 55. I am guessing something to do with his resiratory system, he always had issues with his lungs. Not that it prevented him from smoking but he had quit drinking by the time he passed. Your father had no shortage of demons to contend with thats for sure. He probably considered me one of them but no one is your problem unless you give them that kind of power.

It seemed like it only worked between myself and your father as long as I made all the effort or took all the responsibility for a conflict and that is dysfunctional and toxic both. Today I am unwilling to play as anybody's goon, duncecap, or fool.

Well darling, I gotta go. Can't wait to catch up with you again one day good Lord willing and tempers don't rise.

Love, Mom

_____

_____

_____

"When you get what you want, that's God;'s direction. But when you don't get what you want, that's God's protection."–Unknown

February 2nd, 2020

Dear Riley;

Your older brother looks like you, God showed me in the psych ward. Twenty five years ago in a general hospital I miscarried and was placed in a room with a woman having a real baby that I saw the next morning. Ever since I have been telling God every so often; "I never got to see his face."

Right away when I landed in the main area of what was the wing I would be staying in, an aboriginal kid, about 25 years old who danced and kick boxed imaginary foes stopped, looked at me, drew his upper lip back in a snarl and hiss-mouthed; "You're so f'ing pathetic." It stunned me, we had never met before, not had a conversation muchless a conflict. While I gasped for air he whirled away and was gone.

I began complaining to God about him in my head and those complaints were transformed into prayers for the young man. I noticed his eyes were two black holes in his head. Rumor was he was schizophrenic. "He is one of our sickest," the nurse that saw the altercation told me. "But I can assure," he is not dangerous." OOOO I thought. I don't know about that. He seems plenty dangerous to me. And just like that I judged him, a trait I love to hate in people.

I kept praying—well kabitzing about him really, to God, and this amazing sensation happened. Like all the finest melted gold, butter, and oil in the world poured over my head at the same time, covering mee in warmth. I couldn't wipe the grin off my face and every time we passed he was flowing, rippling or punching someone imaginary, but I sensed he could see me. The next time I saw him at the same area where he had told me off, I asked him; "do you need to use the phone?" He who was said to be non communicative for the most part, looked at me, then forced the word out in a monotone; "NO." Progress! I thought, excited. In the dining room immediatley after, I caught him staring at me across the room with a puzzled expression as if to say: "what's with her?!" The next time he walked by me I noticed his eyes had fleshed out and they shone slightly now from the two empty holes they had been. I realized God was at work and amped up my prayers, not that poor old God needed my help, but maybe, just maybe, I needed to be part of this.

He moved by the television one day glanced up at it and laughed. An actual mirthful laugh. And now on top of love God poured out a little pride on me, pride like a mother of a newborn.

Then the day came when something was very different— I shivered and said; "Brrrr, brrr," and he heard me and laughed, then imitated me. "Brrrr, brrrr." They kept the hospital so cold.

Then the big day came when he was no longer Tarzan or George of some imaginary jungle and walking a straight line fit to beat Johnny Cash. I didn't even clue in at first, I looked and looked at him and thought, "something's different, something's different." Aha! He is walking! My boy is walking!

"Isn't he something?" God spoke up just then. "Yes actually," I agreed where once I thought I would not. "Yeah," I could feel God smiling, which is hard to describe. "He is one of mine– I just love him so much. But he also looks like one of yours."

Huh?! Now God had my full attention. "Yes, you said you never got to see Bailey's face. Well I still save two of everything."

"That's what my son looks like?!" I was credulous. "But he is dark...the father was a blue eyed blonde like me."

"He is an eighth aboriginal," God reminded me. "I took that color and I magnified it– I colored outside the lines for you." And I instantly knew what he was talking about. When I was four I was beaten for coloring outside the lines. God gave me back a double portion just like he promises in scripture.

Ooooo, my son is a lady killer...angel killer? I will figure something out, haha. I might have known he was like one of my kids when he shot me all that attitude, lol.

When you grow up mennonite/german and live in a sea of blue eyes and blonde hair you develop a partiality to brown hair and brown eyes. You are here because someone was tall, dark and handsome.

That being said I do not endorse relationships based on looks, it is shallow. I have been told by men; "I love you, you're beautiful." I replied; "then find another reason to love me because beauty fades, dumb is forever." (Quote from Judge Judy) I could be in some real trouble here...haha. Love, Mom

_____

_____

_____

"See, I have engraved you on the palms of my hands; your walls are ever before me. Your sons hasten back, and those who laid you waste depart from you. Lift up your eyes and look around; all your sons gather and come to you." Isaiah 49:16-18(NIV).

February 3rd, 2020

Dear Riley;

Since I got out of the hospital I have been haunted by that verse. The weird thing is to that after the nervous breakdown, I have been more flighty, more blonde, you might say. But that verse dogged me until I asked God "why? What are you trying to tell me?" Especially the part: "your sons hasten back..."

"There were others," he said. "The two miscarriages while pregnant with Riley...there were others. Two boys. And they look like their father too."

And just like that I was in the anger stage of grief: "I have three sons?!" (Not here). "You couldn't have left me one son?! Sons look after their mothers! And look at what my daughters did! Betrayed me! You couldn't leave me with ONE SON?" I have even seen a step son look after his step mother.

He let me rip and roar for a while and then I asked;

"what are there names?" Well, Bailey I knew, I named Bailey Jean myself and then took the name to carry him, the only way I knew how.

"You tell me," He said quietly. Isaiah 43:4 (NIV) says; "since you are precious and honored in my sight, and because I love you…" God honored me as a mother. No judgement over the fornication or whathaveyou. I picked the names: "Denver Carlyle and Miles Emile," for your brothers.

I have no trouble remembering your hateful words to me, calling your own mother a skank, the c-word, worthless c-word, wishing me a slow death of a cancer and so on.

In the verse it says; "those who laid you waste depart from you…" you are even in that verse as a destroyer. I pray for you when my heart isn't numb. I ask for deliverance from evil and for your reconciliation to God, even if never to me. That is how much I have had to let go of you.

If God didn't carry me like a baby himself I would be a grease stain on the sidewalk. Love, Mom

_____

_____

_____

"I have so much to do that I shall spend the first three hours in prayer." —Martin Luther King

"What God expects us to achieve he enables us to accomplish." —Stephen Olford

February 4th, 2020

Dear Riley;

Ever notice how one never has to wait to slide into a ditch? No applying and waiting six to eight weeks... haha.

I looked around the second hand stores and antique shops for items that remind me of you. That seems to be where there'll be dreamcatchers and prints of aboriginal artwork, not the grocery store, lol. Lately the dream catchers have looked shabby though.

Do you remember when I went busking at the smaller farmer's market in "R————?" And it was for money to go towards your field trip to New York so you stood beside me and plucked the proceeds out of the accordian case as fast as they came, lol. We did well.

The first meal you sat down to eat with your dad in a restuarant on the way to La Loche to meet the family tree, he was struggling to eat with missing teeth and you happily plucked french fries off of his plate.

We stopped near M at a place in the wilderness that had been a residential school that burned down. It was hard to say what activity there was more of; mosquitoes or spirits. The souls of the unburied are at great unrest there, they have not been properly consecrated nor commemorated. I thought aboriginals were all over that stuff—kind of disappointed actually. It needs to happen. Maybe you will be instrumental in that process.

Lately I have been drumming and I am not a drummer. Makes me wonder if it is the same beat of a drum near you, kind of like looking up at the stars and wondering if you see the same ones I do.

Do you remember going through the Japanese phase? I used to love collecting stuff for you from the second hand store where I worked and where you and Rachel volunteered also to get some work experience.

I wonder what will become of your dads grave plot in Fort Saint John that he prepaid for and obviously never used since he was buried in La Loche. Well annehways...

Love, Mom

_____

_____

_____

"Don't be pushed around by the fears in your mind. Be led by the dreams in your heart." -Roy T. Bennett

February 5th, 2020

Dear Riley:

There are many repeats in this book. Repetition is the language of the traumatized soul. Oddly, the same goes for healing. Rapid Eye Movement Desensitization reprocessing therapy is something I thought was too simple to work and it was repetitious also. By bringing up a traumatic memory and rolling my eyes like a teenager, then breathing deeply I was able to regain alot of my short term memory.

I miss reading bedtime stories to my little girls, one head on each of my shoulders, a dark one and a light one.

The catalogue I shop too much from has a disney character charm bracelet that you liked. They also still have the ring for your sedona sky set. I would like to get that for you before they stop producing it so I can give it to you one day. That is also the shopaholic in me that wants to believe I am fixing something with spending and I know I am not. The first step is admitting it.

You said once you wanted to join the police force, or a police force. I wonder if you still do.

Gotta go. Love, Mom

_____

_____

_____

"You most effective ministry will come out of your deepest hurts."-Rick Warren

"Other people will find healing in your wounds."-Rick Warren.

February 6th, 2020

Dear Riley;

Today was a cry day, for a variety of reasons. Just about knocked my denture loose, haha. I always carry some degree of pain over you into every circumstance.

We used to see-saw, you and I, whenever it was time to go anywhere you would run for one more thing and so I would do something while I waited for you and back and forth we'd go. Then we'd get mad at each other for making each other late, lol. A well oiled, sputtering machine we were. Totally flooded.

Today it was reinforced once again like I learned in first grade...boys are yucky. Lol. Men, as you will remember, have not been a good thing in my life, no matter how hard I tried to make them so. I give up.

It would be so much fun to put a treasure hunt together for you again. Remember I did it for your 16th birthday in the basement apartment. You have even sent the rings back that I gave you. Which I have then packed up send back to you. Roundie roundie.

I feel like I missed so much of your life. There are so many regrets...

Maybe instead of my trying to buy happiness and fix things with the whole shopping journey, the next time I see you we will make gifts to catch up with each other. Just like the crafts we did when you were little and it was just the two of us.

Come back soon and be little again, willya?

Mommy loves you.

_____

_____

_____

"In the end, we will remember not the words of our enemies but the silence of our friends."–Martin Luther King Junior

February 7th, 2020

Dear Riley;

Another cry day. Yay for consistency. Even though God is going to restore you back to me, the day isn't here yet so I cry. Hell hath no torment like the grief of a mother.

At the second hand store I found a pair of brand new crocheted booties, pink with darker pink bows and bought them. I used to have little pink moccasins for you...

You will always be my little girl in my mind. I will see my baby in your face always.

Wow this is hard. Could the pain weigh anymore? And yet I am not experiencing anything I haven't done to God. He has the same kind of children we do.

You're going to do so well, Riley, you're such a little ambassador. God will use your passion. Your Mama didn't raise quitters nor fools, somehow. Haha. Well God, please give her a big hug from me tonight. Squish her.

Stroke her left eyebrow so she will relax and fall asleep.
Amen.

Someone once said it is harder to be an atheist than
to believe in God. I wonder if it is the same for people
trying not to love someone they love.

Well it didn't take long to hate living in a small town
again. Everyone in your business. You get your blood
tested at the hospital and then by the time you walk to
the hardware store they are discussing the results on
aisle nine. The trick is probably just to not give a rip.
I stuck some letters on the back of my car that spell
out: "If they chase you out of town, act like you are
leading the parade." Translation; up yours.

Brennan Manning said: "christianity is a lonely
house on a windy hill." Because even so -called other
believers will cause you pain. Christians are some of
the most evil people you will ever meet. So if I pray
someone will come to the Lord I always add: "please let
them TRULY be saved." In this town, they are extra
holy. Me too! Me too. Wait for me! Sarcasm.

Lol. Love Mom

_____

_____

_____

"She is clothed with strength and dignity; she can laugh at the days to come." Proverbs 31:25 (NIV).

February 8th, 2020

Dear Riley;

When you and Rachel moved out you really scalped me in linen and dishes, lol. I am just now getting some stuff back together. Oh—and you broke up sets too. Bah humbug!

T and I are split up for the last time. You saw him as a father figure and he is a good dad. Maybe one day you will reconnect with him. I am just sorry my love life reads like a white man's fishing licence: catch and release only.

It has been thirty years since males have first started screwing me around. I always say I can't even develop a crush without getting burned, but I guess it's time to stop saying that. A person should really watch what they think and say both.

I am suggesting to grieving people that they write a journal to their missing loved one to help. It seems to work. The cheapest form of therapy really is a notebook and a pen.

Oh Riley...my prayer is that you come to the end of yourself and find that God lives there. Big Daddy loves you and he is the real hero of your life. I pray you will hear his voice again.

Love, Mom

_____

_____

_____

The Starfish Poem

A little boy walked carefully

along a crowded beach

where starfish by the hundreds

lay there within his reach

They washed up with each rippling wave

as far as the eye could see

And each starfish was sure to die

if they were not sent back to sea

So one by one he rescued them

then they heard a stranger call

"It won't really make a difference

for you cannot save them all."

But as he tossed yet another one

back toward the ocean's setting sun

He answered with deep compassion;

"I made the difference for that one!"

Author Unknown

"I cannot do all the good that the world needs. But the world needs all the good that I can do." -Jana Stanfield

"If your compassion does not include yourself, it is incomplete." -Jack Cornfield

February 9th, 2020

Dear Riley;

Is there anyone "normal," left on the planet, I wonder? Everywhere I go, everyone seems so screwed up. Guess that means we are in good company, all of us, and normal has slipped away for the greater good of the crowd of misfits.

On a much happier note, legends say that humming-birds float free of time, carrying our hopes for love, joy and celebration. The hummingbird's delicate grace reminds us that life is so rich, beauty is everywhere, every personal connection has meaning and that laughter is life's sweetest creation. Yay hummingbirds.

Lately I have been going to alot of church. It seems to help with the emotional pain. Which we all have some of and I have purchased in bulk.

Men are still boys and boys are still yucky, what else can I say...today I made my love life God's problem and felt loads better about it.

I pray you come back from the kingdom of darkness everyday practically. God says he will do it; deliver you from evil. Hallelujah.

This year I am publishing my trilogy, Growing Up Mennonite. Exciting.

You called me an uneducated @#$% in one of your hate emails. Well the fourty grand in student loans I have beg to differ, and me I don't beg I just differ. All the time actually.

I have always loved learning and taken every course I could. I fought to get you your status card which will pay for education for the rest of your life if nothing changes. The student loans were a huge ordeal to get and by the time I got them I was usually in such duress I had to drop out of school and use them as debt consolidation for unpaid bills that had piled up while they fiddled around.

There are also different kinds of smarts and book smart will not be the be all end all for you. Love, Mom

_____

_____

_____

"But God chose the foolish things of the world to shame the wise; God chose the weak things of the world to shame the strong." I Cor. 1:27(NLT).

February 10th, 2020

Dear Riley;

"The world needs more people like who God created you to be."

I see you everywhere some days. I found a little Minnie Mouse pin in my jewelry box that I could not recall buying but it reminded me of you when you were born. So I pinned it to a card that looks a Navajo blanket and stuck it with the package I am sending your way.

When we were Seventh Day Adventists, we had left the main core church and attended the one in someone's living room in Chimeny Valley. One day the lesson was on King Nebachadnezer. You piped up:"In Veggietales? King Nebachadnezer was a pickle." They almost had to carry me outta there laughing as hard as I did. After that though, I got rid of the veggie tales series, haha.

I hope that if you ever read this journal, that it doesn't just fuel your anger toward me.

There are two empty bedrooms upstairs I am slowly decorating. They are spare rooms but I wish they contained my little girls.

The effects of the nervous breakdown are still very much present despite the fact that I bounced back to reality and wanting to live...the short term memory that I had regained with EMDR therapy has slipped backward a little. There are still lots of pages missing from my book, mentally speaking. I still blank out. It will take time.

It sucks to be attractive enough to make trouble but not enough to make a living at it, haha. Women sometimes still take one look at me and act jealous, and the odd married man makes as much trouble as he can. As opposed to people just learning to be happy with themselves and their lives. Or getting a gym pass and plucking something.

The concept of bored married men I do not understand. They climax alot easier and more often...woman have to permanently traumatize their bodies to have the babies from those encounters...and the MEN get bored?! I have zero sympathy. We get bored too and hey-if you want heavy breathing breathe heavy. Such wisdom, lol. Love, Mom

"My heroes have always killed cowboys." (Just kidding)–
Unknown, paraphrased from title of Willie Nelson song

February 11th, 2020

Dear Riley:

I have had more children after my hysterectomy than I
ever did when I still had a uterus. I drove a schoolbus,
now I am a Sunday school teacher for the second time
in a row. Cool huh?

This week my class is going to build alters out of actual
stones as we cover the Elijah story. Apparently they
have to be constructed out of twelve stones. Now aren't
you glad you know that? Haha.

Isn't it great having a dog, then when you pass gas
you can blame it on him...What?! I started a new
paragraph...

Joke: how do you stop a man from attacking you? (Ask
him for a commitment).

It's hard to have only one of five children in my life
who have passed through my body. Your oldest brother
must have been the good child, lol. Pardon my rough
sense of humor–it is how I cope.

Since you went to public school you became obsessed with
your aboriginal heritage. It was taught. They had no
special classes of activities for the Muslims, Spanish,

Germans, Caucasions, etc. Just the Aboriginals. When will people realize that treating people like you need to apolgize to them for who they are IT'S STILL RACISM. Anyway, the Bible says: "Bride of the King, listen to what I say-forget about your people and your relatives." Psalms 45:10 (NIV). Look who Jesus had in his lineage, a prostitute, a murdering adulterer (King David). It never stopped, defined, nor fueled His purpose.

Love, Mom

_____

_____

_____

"He who makes no mistakes makes nothing."—Unknown

February 12th, 2020

Dear Riley;

A really good scripture verse is Isaiah 54:5; "For your maker is your husband, the Lord of hosts is His name; and the Holy one of Israel is your Redeemer, the God of the whole earth He is called." I am Mrs. Lord of hosts, address; the Almighty Dwelling Place, as per Psalm 91: 1 and 2 (NIV) "Whoever dwells in the shelter of the Most High will rest in the shadow of the Almighty, I will say of the Lord, He is my refuge and my fortress, my God, in whom I trust.

And because the earth is the Lord's, it doesn't matter whose land it is, because at the end of the long hard day, it all belongs to God. The whole earth is a rental home and we're "just a passing through" like the Jim Reeves song.

Do you remember when we had to shave your dogs butt to keep him clean and you declared; "he has just lost all his dignity!" We laughed and laughed.

There was this amazing guy in the hospital when I was there; it was like he was reborn when he discovered some psychological truths about having been sexually abused. He became "the well-mart greeter" of the psychward. He told me; "get rid of that negativity," more than once. The truth can only set one free, and that was truth.

One day "wellmart" came running into the dining hall repeating, "it's f—ed. It's f—-ed, it's f—ed.!" He had been readng a book about sexual abuse that triggered him a little. I said in true German somber sarcasm, "I'm guessing it is f-ed?"

Oh Father God, I just pray you would redeem (to be made useful for the kingdom of light) my daughter for the works you have prepared in advance for her to do. (Ephesions 2:10) Don't leave her in the kingdom of darkness. I plead the blood of Jesus over her soul. Thank you and amen.

Love, Mom

_____

_____

_____

"I tried to keep an open mind but then my brains fell out."-Unknown

February 13th, 2020

Dear Riley;

It's Valentine's Day tomorrow and here I am, moving furniture. Yay me. It appears as if P.T.S.D. gives one incredible rage and I have learned to channel it to move heavy objects by myself, lol.

I wonder if you have a date tomorrow.

For nearly three decades I have been cursing and now I am trying to quit and it is so hard. I have even changed the a-word to calling someone an "a-type personality minus the organizational skills." And I say: "what the fridge magnet?!" But it it a hard habit to quit.

And I do note that I have been cussing and swearing as long as I have been looking for a man. Coincidence? No.

"Addiction is that thing that makes you fail in your responsibilities," they said at your graduation. I have a theory though, that the ability to be addicted is a good thing if we get hooked on good behaviors and patterns.

Love, Mom

_____

_____

_____

"Since you are precious and honored in my sight, and because I love you, I will give men in exchange for you, and people in exchange for your life." Isaiah 43:4 NIV

February 14th, 2020

Dear Riley;

Happy Valentine's Day, kidlet. This used to be the hundredth day of school that caused teachers to demand kids to bring 100 of something to stress out the parents, lol.

I texted; "Happy V-Day," to your sister which cracked us up because it sounded like an S.T.D.

Grandpa K likes to tell stories and jokes and he always laughs at his own comics. He tells about a bear who met up with a hunter and whaddya know they both spoke english. The hunter admits he has been looking for a fur coat and the bear says he wants a full stomach. They resolve it, and only the bear comes out of the forest.

It is alarming to look back and realize how many abusive men I have known. And to pray for a revolution among men for healing and deliverance. Hurt people hurt people. Love, Mom

"Maybe you have to know the darkness before you can apreciate the light." – Madeleino L'Engle

February 15th, 2020

Dear Riley;

I miss the days when you loved me and I was your hero.

You were always an obstinate little stinker, man! You probably still don't do anything you don't want to.

Everytime I mess with jewelry I think of you. I keep old pieces to repair better pieces with.

When I was ten or eleven years old I made a portrait on a piece of plywood using pencil crayons, no easy feat with soft wood, but I did it. Today, decades later, I realized it was your face I created against the backdrop of a stained glass church window. Ofcourse it is long gone. But I wonder if I could do it again.

I get rid of stuff so fast. It's driven by a deep psychological scar that drives it; loss. And culling stuff at my discretion promises to restore some kind of control. It's about being in control of my losses to compensate for all the times I lost something where I wasn't in control.

May God heal us all. Amen. Love, Mom

_____

_____

"If they treat you like a joke, leave them like its funny."–Unknown

February 16th, 2020

Dear Riley;

Do you remember your step-grandma from the marriage to the Seventh Day Adventist? A drama queen on energy drinks spiked with steroids, holy moly. Forgive me Lord but yikes.

There is a joke about how a preacher got into a fender bender and the other guy ripped and cursed and swore at him. When he was done the pastor spoke up and said; "well, I am a man of the God and I can't use the language you did, but when you get home I hope your mother runs out from under the porch and bites you."

When you were between the ages of seven to nine you were a gifty little giver, always thrusting a gift into someone's hand. Usually it was something you had made yourself. A crafty gifty kid you were.

Miss You Lots, hugs, love Mom

_____

_____

_____

"No matter what happens, no matter how far you seem to be away from where you want to be, never stop believing that you will somehow make it." —Unknown.

February 17th, 2020

Dear Riley;

Every time I was involved with an aboriginal man he cheated on me. Do you like how I worked that into the situation? Your dad had three women going at a time, something he later admitted to me. That was my lot in life when it came to men; cheaters and beaters. The body may have changed a few times, but it seemed to always be the same guy.

I know your inner child wants and needs Daddy to be a hero but in truth, he did not live a stellar lifestyle. He worked hard and he played even harder. His artwork was beautiful and liked to laugh, but he was no gentleman. The truth may irritate you and even inconvienence the crap out of you, but it will also set you free.

You know in all of what I have told you about your pop; the Bible says honor your father and your mother. Not just your good father and mother. Love, Mom

_____

_____

_____

"When God pushes you to the edge of difficulty, trust Him. Either He will catch you when you fall or He will teach you how to fly." -Unknown

February 18th, 2020

Dear Riley;

When you were just a matter of weeks old, I rushed you to the doctor, convinced you had pneumonia. It turned out to be nasal congestion.

I tried to boil the world so you would not experience sickness or disease, lol. First time parent.

Today I remembered when you were about three to five you decided you were scared of Dr. Seuss's Zizzer Zazzer Zuzzes and prayed every night for protection of them. Lol. Those big scary purple and white quilted plaid guys.

Rachel used to pray; "Surround me with angels and help me not to be afraid." Now she says she is an atheist. Says her Daddy is a hero and God is a deadbeat father. I would say she has them reversed but it isn't for me to fix.

It's pleasant when good memories come up. I am grateful for those and for the gift of motherhood. Love, Mom

_____

_____

_____

"Don't put a coma where God put a period."—Unknown

February 19th, 2020

Dear Riley:

Sometimes I wear your birthstone on a ring to remember you as I go along, my pearly girly.

I remember when you went through the "Joseph," phase, as in the movie. That video played and played until one had it memorized and heard it when it was off. You and Rachel acted out parts of it.

Sometime, once you are back in my life and with all your training, you could maybe help decipher why the world seems to make excuses for men. It's like, a woman leaves a man and he says; "what's wrong with her?" Meanwhile she is asking herself; "what's wrong with me?"

Joke: "What do a thousand battered women have in common?" (They didn't listen).

There's a joke; "what is the first thing a woman does when she comes home from the women's shelter?" Answer: the dishes, if she knows what is good for her.

Love, Mom

_____

_____

_____

People judge.

God forgives.

Consequences stay.

—Me

February 20th; 2020

Dear Riley;

You were born fighting for air and you have been fighting ever since, Warrior Princess. It explains a lot of things.

When you were 3 you said you wanted to be a "princess/angel," for halloween. So you wore wings with your royalty dress that I added eyelet lace to and a gold tinsel/clothes hanger halo instead of a crown.

Around the same age whenever we had to get ready to go somewhere you said; "just wait I'm getting organDized." Lol.

We were all over the road on what stance to take on Halloween because I was undecided....It was wrong it was okay...back and forth. My bad.

Our family pictures have all the negatives and proofs conglomerated onto discs for you and your sister. If someone knows how to do that. A specialty shop maybe.

There is a gazillion apps that are supposed to convert your old negatives into pictures but so far I have not been successful in finding one that actually works.

A man goes to the doctor and says: "doctor doctor, everywhere I touch myself it hurts." The doctor says; "you must have a broken finger." As his counsellor I would tell him he also had a victim mentality.

Lol. Love, Mom

_____

_____

_____

"What's broken can be mended. What hurts can be healed. And no matter how dark it gets, the sun is going to rise again."—Unknown

February 27th, 2020

Dear Riley;

They say to ask why is the language of a victim, so try not to ask it. And being a victim just means you are not in control, that things happen to you, people do things to you.

Some other wise person also said the person asking the questions is the one in control, the individual doing all the talking is not.

You used to hardly ever get sick until you got your vaccinations all caught up when you were fifteen. Then you caught everything going. Yay vaccinations. Talk about robbing Peter to pay Paul, get treated for one to bring on another.

I remember reading in Psalms somewhere once..."have mercy on me for men hotly pursue me..." It's like..."that's enough mercy Lord. Really."

Well I can't talk a lot about you because I don't know what you are doing and I am done jawing about me.

It saddens me how the church has damaged people with their message about sex. Besides the pastor that I heard say; "sex within marriage is the only safe sex," which made me cringe because my brief marriage involved abuse of every kind, the "sex is bad," note ruins people, in my opinion. You cannot feed the sex-is-bad-wrong-dirty-until-you-are-married-message and then people get married and go do this bad thing that is now somehow supposed to be good. Oh, the local puritans that remain single will claim they are waiting for God's person to show up but the truth is, you cannot turn this bad thing around in your mind overnight after a lifetime of negative notations about it. Just my theory. There has to be a better way. The truth is God designed sex to implement His relationship with his bride/any real christian. God's spirit enters us by our choice not His force and unifies us both; the believer to God and vice versa. The Bible says for a man to treat his wife like his own body, and well? He isn't going without satisfaction...

Goodnight!

Love, Mom

_____

_____

_____

"Alpha females don't run in packs. Keeps her circle small. Knows her power and works in silence." –Unknown

February 22nd, 2020

Dear Riley;

This respiratory flu gives the impression I have a buffalo standing on every sinew, fibre, atom, and molecule. I wonder if you have it too. Perhaps we are sharing an experience and don't know it. Yay flu! I miss when you kids were little and climbing in bed with me. Miss the tickling, the giggling and the bedtime stories.

Last summer I tried to go get a restraining order after one of your vendetta benders of hate spamming me with emails. The judge said get an address for service, and I wondered where in your baby book I would paste the document. In the end I just gave up on it, but I know now I can ask for permission to create a facebook page and serve you that way. Tough love is tough but if it has to be done…my human rights to a peaceful life has not expired yet. They don't either. I love you kid, but there could be rough consequences ahead for you. Especially if you harass someone else the way you have me. Sooner or later, someone isn't going to take that kind of treatment and you will get into legal trouble.

Love, Mom

"The language of faith is not please but thank you."–Unknown

February 23rd, 2020

Dear Riley;

I don't actually mind you calling me by my first name. Most people that disrespect me do that much.

Somewhere I read that; "a girl that doesn't respect her mother has no respect for anyone." I agree but that is on you.

Oh the sun is shining so brightly on the cold winter dampness of melting and refreezing. Your dad had a wicked allergy to snow mold and I have a medicocre one. One has to be grateful though, and be thankful the climate here is rather non-conducive to reptiles so that's good.

If you had not already figured as much, the relationship between your father and I was a volatile one and it only worked as long I took all the responsibility. On one of the times he rejected and cold-shouldered you I radically went to bat for you; tore him a third nostril really: "You don't have a fatherly bone in your body except the bone that keeps making you a father." He wasn't a good parent. He abandoned you more than once, cut you off and whatnot. My wish, or hopes and prayers rather, for you and Rachel is that you would truly see your fathers for who and what they were, then forgive and love them anyway. Realistically. Because loving some perfect guy; some hero in your head isn't love at all it is fantasy.

Love, Mom

_____

_____

_____

"The creative adult is the child that survived."
—Unknown

February 24th, 2020

Dear Riley;

Well today was most decidedly a Monday. I almost lost my religion and I am not religious. The wheels came off whatever I touched and then some. Such a wearying of the soul.

I wonder how long it will take before you come back.

Tomorrow is my 44th birthday, yay and yippee. Woot woot. Well, I will see Rachel for lunch anyway; she is such a little workaholic I hardly ever see her. All three of us seem to be, even when I am not employed full time I seem to go and go. My home has to look a certain way…etc. Your Gramma K was like that too.

You know hatred and unforgiveness are like drinking poison and hoping the other guy dies. Jesus forgave the people that were crucifying him as they did it. That is not where I am at, I struggle for a long time to forgive someone. The good Lord didn't ask us to do anything easy, that's for sure.

I remember when I first took you to La Loche to meet your other family tree. We stopped near M where a residential school had burned down and while your dad and I set up camp at one point I stood shivering behind him and he took off his jacket and ordered me to put it on. That was how he was, he read people. The site was riddled with mosquitoes and we hardly slept at all between them and the spiritual unrest. It was like there was a constant prow-wow going on only it was dusk and you could not see anyone responsible for the racket. We gave up in the early morning and just packed up and left. Another long drive later we arrived in pot-holed La Loche where you just walked into your Gramma's arms. Like you two had rehearsed it.

What a place it was, the furthest part of Saskatchewan. Streets of potholes and most people driving a truck. Weathered chipboard on the outside of your Grandmother's house. But so clean- you could have eaten off of any part of it. She was no slouch in the homemaking department either. I had great respect and even a connection with her despite the vast cultural differences. Well, until you decided to bomb that bridge.

Life in a small town continues to be typical. Three thousand other people seem to know more about my life than I do, haha. I like stepping outside and hearing cows mooing in the feedlot. It's a blast from a farmgirls past, but when this guy asked me; "you're a farmgirl right?" I wanted to say bite me. I am many things and the question seemed to come from a "put you in my life where I want you," stance when I wasn't auditioning for a part in his charmed world.

What bugs me a little is the: "this is the world," attitude around here. Gotta go. Love, Mom

_____

_____

_____

"If they're talkin' about you they're leavin everyone else alone."—Unknown

Me: "yeah, well I'm about to charge for that service."

"...they have to talk about you. Because when they talk about themselves, nobody listens."—Unknown

Dear Riley;

February 25th, 2020

I hope and pray you are going to be delivered of anger towards me.

You I almost had your father's name tattooed on my arm. We felt that solid once. Now I am thinking, if I ever get married again, I want my wedding vows tatooed on my inner left arm. Maybe even at the ceremony. If we both did it.

Today is the day...and I have been stressed out...we had lunch which was nice. Rachel was tired from working her eighty hours a week but we took a fairly nice picture. For me tired is just my look so we had us a theme going.

This town continues to try and get its foot on my neck with their judgemental stares; no one ever lets you feel good about yourself in a small community. Well I have got news for them; when it comes to feeling good about myself I won't be asking anybody's permission.

I must go but remember:

If they treat you like a joke, leave them like its funny.

If they chase you out of town act like you're leading the parade. Author unknown

Lol.

Love, Mom

_____

_____

_____

"Don't ever diminish the power of words. Words move hearts and hearts move limbs." —Hamza Yusuf

February 26th, 2020

Dear Riley:

I wish we could be friends now, with boundaries. Maybe one day in the future. I am learning that God only changes what you give him, so I am giving him my life.

You have to get rid of your anger and the bitterness for your own sake. Don't let me be the invisible cancer that eats you alive. To quote Vince Gill; "there ain't no future in the past."

Gratitude is a powerful force along with letting go of the negativity. That which doesn't kill you only makes you more alive in Christ and one can always be grateful for the strength building excercise every hardship has been.

September was always a hard month for us three; everything would be starting up at school and there was countless fees and paperwork to sign if you didn't have the fees. If I was working we were still the working poor.

There is a designated gift stash drawer in the house for you now. Not that I want to be regarded as a money giver or treat holder, just like I used to always tell you when you were younger.

It was so cute when you and Rachel figured out that taxes made the price of things change so in the stores you would spend your allowance but if you only had enough for the sticker price, you would ask; "Mom, if I buy this, will you pay my tax?" We sure developed a familial addiction to the dollar store huh. A team effort.

Lol. Love, Mom

_____

_____

_____

"No person can hold you back when God has decided to raise you up!"–Unknown

February 27th, 2020

Dear Riley;

"Repetition is the language of a wounded child," someone once told me. There is alot of that in this journal.

I remember the day you ran away when I tried to pick you up from school. Then at the youth shelter, you immediatley offered me a gift you had crafted and I froze. I could not bring myself to reach out and accept it. It was a dream catcher you made in crafts shortly after you got there I guess.

It's hard to say but I don't have alot of good memories of you. After age nine especially. It's like the teenage years were always in gear, there was always a problem of some kind, you were a constant pusher of the envelope.

When we moved it R---- you really went downhill. Hormones kicked in, you got your period at age 11 and the entire world was just a few steps away. One day you didn't come home after school and I had to call the police and report a missing child. You were eleven. They sat in their cars forever, running my name first.

I spanked you with an open hand and you and the school counsellor cooked up that I was beating you. That and other stories of abuse from your boyfriends seem to have become your entire identity. Tell me, who are you when the aboriginal nationality and bull crap victim stories are striped away? Are you in there? I think so.

Love, Mom

_____

_____

_____

"Gratitude makes sense of our past, brings peace for today, and creates a vision for tomorrow." Melody Beattie

February 28th, 2020

Dear Riley;

Ever notice how the people who screw with you turn around and call you crazy. It's like they are recognizing their own handiwork!

I wish it was safe to tell you things and not have them thrown at me as a weapon at a later point. That has always been the case though, and as one of my prayers for you is a giant reset.

Nothing happens to the christian without God's permission. Isn't that so cool. The devil has to go through God before he can affect us in any way.

Winter is still here like an unwanted, lingering ex-boyfriend. Arrrgh.

You would this crazy old house I live in with all its nooks and crevices.

In a book I read recently, either Rick Warren's Purpose Driven Life or Toxic Faith, it said you can have worry or worship, not both. Man you were always such a worrywart, must have got it from me. Anyway, I've discovered worship trumps fretting any day, and it isn't sitting in a church singing along to the choir. Worship is simply making it about God rather than myself.

Love, Mom

_____

_____

_____

"Keep going. God did not bring you this far to drop you off."—Unknown, slightly paraphrased by me

February 29th, 2020

Dear Riley;

Tomorrow I teach Sunday School again. We are doing the story of Elijah, I don't know how much you would recall of Bible stories from your childhood. Anyway, if I had another baby to name I think I would name her Brooke Cherith, it's so pretty. And it would have to be a girl, then obviously...which I could not do anymore.

My give a blank is busted toward men, finally. I could use the vacation. Although last night there were ten men banging on the door and I eventually had to let them out. Haha.

Does anyone make a true friend anymore, I wonder. People seem fickle and shallow. Not to be negative, I am trying to get rid of that.

Today I wish you were here eating my egg fried rice and giggling about something. You and Rachel and I sitting down together at an actual table for a meal.

There are some people in the church apparently dead set against my teaching Sunday school. Whoopie ding-dong. I heard it through the gossipvine, no one says it to my face, which is good, because what they think of me is none of my business and I'd like to keep it that way.

Love, Mom

_____

_____

_____

"Most folks are about as happy as they make up their minds to be."-Abraham Lincoln

March 1st, 2020

Dear Riley;

Today I prayed all the curses you sent me would return to you. Then I remembered Jesus made himself a curse in order to nullify all curses.

God told me you need your education in the occult or whatever it is your dabbling in so you can testify against it one day.

Just so you know, a mother's prayers trump all other spiritual activity. The devil hasn't got a chance against a praying parent.

You should see all the cute little kids in my class with big brown eyes. They remind me of you. I am a second generation Sunday school teacher, my dad/Grandpa K was one. It is exhausting, maybe I am trying too hard.

I grew up religious, my Grandpa was the deacon of the church we attended which was the equivalent of Bishop elsewhere it seemed, because he seemed to be the go to person. One of my uncles was a pastor and my father the Sunday-school teacher and us children the example. I think there is such a thing as religious addiction and I call it religaholism. I think I see a lot of it around me–

Addiction is practically a family heirloom–and the only one if I keep moving the way I do. On the K side it is definitely religion, on the P side it is alcoholism.

Your Aunt M2 and your Grandma K were both wearing black when they got married. In one of the Laura Ingalls books it says: "married in black you'll wish yourself back." Ha ha. But it has slimming effects...c'mon now. I always looked better in black...a good Mennonite, lol.

So tired. Goodnight.

Love, Mom

_____

_____

_____

"The biggest point of maturity is when you look at your parents and realize they too, have hearts that can be broken."-Unknown

March 2nd, 2020

Dear Riley;

Life seemed surreal those two times you ran away; once at age 11 and once at age 16 with that awful meth addicted boyfriend.

People have asked me over the years of rebellion and behaviours, if you do drugs. And I say no, except that time you smoked so much weed you ended up in the emergency in R---- and my boss was mad at me for having to leave "a site unmanned." Well I had him cover it himself for me so I could run to the hospital, so what was the real issue? "At school they outlawed bullying, at work they just call it management." I have no idea who said that—I only hope I receive grace when readers see that I did not try to abscond anyone else's verbal work as mine, I do try and give proper credit. The trouble is my short term memory...

Today I wondered if life feels surreal when things go really well. I would not know...if it wasn't for hard times I couldn't tell time. But that sounds a lot like the victim mentality I am trying to get rid of.

I hope you know I am crying for you even though I am Ford tough.

Love, Mom

_____

_____

_____

"If you're going through hell, keep going."—Winston Churchill.

March 3rd, 2020

Dear Riley;

Today was such a down day. People may think I am crazy when I say it would have been easier to bury a child once, grieve and have the pain lessen in time than to be estranged. It's the old rip the band aid off quickly theory perhaps. Anything but this.

You know we don't need a lot, just a few good friends and a small corner of the universe working for us. So today I prayed for that to happen, but mostly I prayed for you to be delivered of evil.

Do you ever wish you could do something heroic or do you see yourself that way already? A lot of people seem to be a hero in their own eyes...I think heroism is like the philosopher's stone in Harry Potter— as soon as you want it you are disqualified.

When I drove a school bus, I didn't always reward a child for doing something good. I wanted them to learn that good deed are their own reward so I gave treats intermittently.

Goodnight. Love, Mom

"May you attract someone who speaks your language so you don't have to spend a lifetime translating your soul."–Unknown

March 4th, 2020

Dear Riley;

I wondered today if you would have fared better if I had not been so honest with your step dad that you were not his child. He met me a second time pregnant again, only two months along if that. You didn't even look like me so he wouldn't have had much argument there...then he wouldn't have been so cruel, refusing to take you along when he was mad at me and only took Rachel. I wish I had just lied if it would have done any good. If it had protected you. Not that I endorse lying. I have been one of those people that usually shoots herself in the foot with honesty; telling you if you look fat in your dress. Lol.

Sometimes I wonder if what goes around actually does come around? Like do people actually get what they deserve? Then there is me, wondering if I have truly sown some of the deeds that come my way. The Bible says in Hosea 8:7; "those that sow wind shall reap a whirlwind."

There will be very few family heirlooms in this little family...we were poor so often and moved too much...Oh well. The most important things in life are not things.

Aunt MJ sent a good quote to me yesterday: "Never cry for the person who hurts you, just smile and say; "Thank you for giving me a chance to find someone better than you." Amen to that.

In food safe we learned: "when in doubt throw it out." That should be a rule for dating also: "when in doubt throw the whole dude out."

Recently I either learned or confirmed that church is a good place to be judged and there is total acceptance at an AA meeting. Even if the meeting is held in the church basement; there is acceptance until you move up to the main crowd in the service on the main floor.

Gotta go, goodnight.

Love, Mom

_____

_____

_____

"What lies behind us, and what lies ahead of us, are tiny matters compared to what lies within us."-Ralph Waldo Emerson

March 5th, 2020

Dear Riley;

I agree with the above statement. We codependents look too much to others for what we already have. I heard a joke about being co-dependent-you start drowning and somebody else's life flashes before you.

There is nothing so draining than constantly hearing: "what do you mean?"from your so-called significant other. It's crazy-making behaviour. I was like that.

You can never build any kind of a relationship with a liar. They used to say: you can turn your back on a thief, because you know what he'll do. But never, ever turn your back on a liar...they are unstable. Plus a lie is the simplest form of disrespect.

I have decided I am not forgetful...my brain just has an elaborate privacy act in place in between all transactions. Ha ha.

It is important that you have a spiritual life with the good force; The Light. We are a spoked wagon wheel and need all aspects of our lives taken care of; emotional, sexual, physical, psychological, and spiritual. If not the solid wooden wheel goes flat, lol. Just thought I would throw that in for free...as my friend would say.

Instead of bar hopping like young'uns my gal-pal and are planning to go church hopping and see what's up with the local groups. There is one on every corner here so it could be a while...We will of course, avoid the cults and save some time that way.

It came to me today that I need to repent for picking up some of my issues with my own mother if I want my prayers for my daughter to be answered. Sometimes when I try to walk in forgiveness I stumble. What can I say, I am human.

Love, Mom

_____

_____

_____

"You are so much more than your current trial. It doesn't define you. God is directing you to something greater."–Joel Osteen

March 6th, 2020

Dear Riley;

There is a point where people no longer deserve your time and effort. The Bible says don't cast your pearls before swine, as in, don't feed pearls to piggies, they will only trample on them. It is true. In my terms: don't feel bad when you can't make chicken salad from chicken-something-else…So I culled my membership today and kicked myself for having been so naive as to ever think THAT church would work out. But then again why go anyplace that would have me. I mean what-the?!

The world makes excuses for men and the church kicks it up a notch. What is the logic? Because God is a man therefore all males have one up on women? What about the devil being a male also? Duh, you would think that would help level the score. Or is that Garden of Eve thing where she supposedly misleads him and women have been getting blamed ever since? As if he had no testicular matter to speak of and say no with?!

The base of the cross is an equal playing field. But people forget.

I think some churches are the whore Revelations talks about. "Get everyone in here paying." That is the attitude. Real love-not so much. Of course we are all guilty sinners without exception. We are as bad as the people we complain about.

So anyway, I dumbed down my letter of: count me the bleep out; because they don't get it anyway. Washing water and sawing sawdust is very taxing as is explaining the obvious to people dedicated to hearing only their own agenda. Toxic much?!

I lost my to do list for the year. Typical, but a little stressful...make a list and find the list only to need a map to find the original idea...humbug.

Love, Mom

_____

_____

_____

"Some of us aren't meant to belong. Some of us have to turn the world upside down and shake the----out of it until we make our own place in it."–Elizabeth Lowell.

March 7th, 2020

Dear Riley;

You are like that, you were never one of the crowd and you got that from me. Sucks to be you maybe. We are truly on this planet to make a difference not to make friends. And when you make a difference you won't only make friends. To change the world you cannot be crippled with worry about who likes you and who doesn't. They don't have to like you...they just have to respect you. And vice versa. Never ask for or demand something you aren't willing to give yourself. That's hypocrisy and another paragraph...

I sure won't miss all the breeding the talk thereof in that stinking church. Bunch of Mennonites. And then let the kids run amok, because people are having babies for how they are made not for the responsibility thereof. Makes me sick, but perhaps I was a little bit of a drill sergeant as a parent. But ya ain't nobody around there unless you're barefoot squatting baby dispenser or a potential one. I mean how else are they gonna expand the church?! That's thinking.

I will never forget the prayer request to pray for a females twiddle-twaddle because it wasn't healing right from the last, umpteenth baby she had in her forties. I found myself yelling at my phone-thank God the google sound was off-"Of course your hee-who isn't healing! It was not meant to be a main highway!" Even more bizarre, the last kid had not even taken the main highway, it had to be dragged out of her abdomen. So it did not even make sense...Nothing like praying specifically I guess. Personally I would just have requested prayer for health issues, I wouldn't have named body parts, not those anyway. Hee hee.

Well tomorrow's another day, ha ha.

Love, Mom

_____

_____

_____

"When it is not God's time you cannot force it. When it is in God's time, you cannot stop it." –Unknown

March 8th, 2020

Dear Riley;

You used to lick the last piece of cake you wanted or lick your finger and stroke the slice you wanted and prohibited everyone else from taking it. Cute. I wish you were here right now and I would bake a cake for you.

This journal might be the only one of its kind, despite what I wrote in the original cover: "The Book of Riley," volume one. I am not writing it to be politically or emotionally correct, but to process my pain, and hopefully make an amend to you.

I have felt like dying, living without you. Losing your brother, Bailey, prepared me for this though. Every lousy event in life prepares you for another. That which doesn't kill you only makes you more alive in Christ, and for that I am truly grateful.

Bye for now, Tweedle.

Love, Mom

_____

_____

_____

"Even if you win the rat race you're still a rat." –Unknown

March 9th, 2020

Dear Riley:

Twenty four years ago I left your abusive step father and went to a women's shelter, pregnant with you. We passed him in the van one day and he looked dazed and crestfallen that I had left him after he demanded I have an abortion. Sadly it would not be my last stay in a women's shelter...it bothers me when people judge me for having had so many relationships. I have had to flee and hide for my life. There was nothing to work out with drunks, cheaters and beaters. Except to stop choosing them and believing they would change and become what I wanted and thought I needed. Was I hoping or joking?!

It's an odd coincidence too that I left him for the first time on March 9th, and statistics say an a woman leaves a man an average nine times before she leaves him for the last time.

In so many ways I have had to let go of the life I signed on for and accept what is.

Rachel tells me you are tiny now. Well, you kinda came that way...all your life you have plumped up and stretched out alternately.

You have lived your life the way you were born also fighting for air then fighting everything all the time even when it wasn't necessary. I hope one day you will pick your battles. Goodness knows I sucked at it.

On one hand little things matter more now and I don't mean pointless arguments. Since the nervous breakdown and hospitalization I have noticed my feet hitting the frozen sidewalk in boots in the wintertime, walking my dog. Mindfulness, they call it in therapy. Paying attention to the small details to gain your grip on life again.

Sometimes I still wish I could find the love of my life and have the ultimate romance when the truth is I should have given up on men years ago. And Jesus is the lover of my soul. I have sung the line "Love divine all loves excelling," from the old hymn often. It still frustrates me to be created a certain way and not be able to live it, and I don't mean that I need a man to help me survive. Never had that never will. The heart has no brains I guess, so how do you stop wanting what you have always wanted? It's like a woman who can't have children but wants them. Well I can check that off.

Love, Mom

_____

_____

_____

"The day you stop racing is the day you win the race."
Buddha Teas.

March 10th, 2020

Dear Riley;

You were back. You were RIGHT there. So close I could have reached out and touched you, sitting in arm's reach of me, your hair up in a high ponytail. You needed me for something...and then you were gone because I woke up. Why did I have to wake up. Wakefulness is highly over-rated.

I sure didn't turn out to be the parent I set out to be, and you won't either— but I like to think I did the best I could with what I had at the time.

You are such a little ambassador, unafraid to speak up, to fight for what you believe is right. It's just too bad my mistakes in parenting have become such an identity for you. You are someone without that.

Sometimes I have nightmares you will die young. Call it C.P.T.S.D., call it a mother's intuition, call it what the Bible says about what happens to people that disrespect and dishonour their parents. It is my prayer that you, Rachel and I fulfill any God-given purpose for our lives before the lights go out. And that you turn your life back over to HIM before it is too late.

You might call me a religious fanatic but the truth as I see it; we are all fanatic about something anyway, may as well make it Jesus. And I prefer the term spiritual.

By the way I have rewritten the meaning of the words: Complicated Post Trauma Stress Disorder to mean: Christ's Promises Toward Sustaining Deliverance.

Onwards and upwards;

Love, Mom

_____

_____

_____

"Sometimes things have to fall apart so better things can fall together." -Marilyn Monroe

March 17th, 2020

Dear Riley;

I rewrote the words to the song: On the Wings of a Dove, just for fun and to tell the story of living in H, Alberta surrounded by so called male puritans. The trick is to keep up with the original tune and sing it without cracking up as you sing: "On the Wings of a Snow White Prairie Chicken."

I never went with anyone that actually had anything to his name and I would not have wanted his stuff or money if the relationship hadn't worked out. But I am tired of being broke and I can certainly go broke alone.

In the hospital I apologized to a man on behalf of all the women that try to clean a man out at the breakup. Whatever happened to; "your money's no good here?!" I always do a cleanse after a breakup- get rid of whatever gift or artifact still reminds me of the failed relationship, I don't want anything to remind me of it. Now there is new law called "unlawful enrichment," translated; "you greedy b---." Some men have done it to women now-taken more than their share of the combined assets. What bugs me is seeing the marriages that are only really held together by fear and money.

"I don't want him/her to have my half." Okay...but you each have half now. Duh. Fifty percent starts when the marriage does, not once unhappiness kicks in. If people could just realize that.

As a result of the way I process things— eliminating items that trigger pain...there is little left of you and Rachel's childhoods. Mostly pictures. In the hurting moms support group I joined the leader warned repeatedly: "don't throw out your pictures."

There was a time I couldn't even look at family photos, let alone put them up. Now they are up. I'll take progress anyway I can get it.

Love, Mom

_____

_____

_____

"Lack of forgiveness causes almost all of our self-sabotaging behaviour."–Unknown

March 12th, 2020

Dear Riley;

I have learned to watch out for people who fall all over themselves trying to befriend you; cuz in the next breath they are falling all over themselves trying to destroy you.

Blank days are harder than cry days. The ones where I can't remember much about your life...and I wonder if I have failed to forgive you and myself for the nature of our relationship. Pain provides...in a bizarre way. It is why I asked God not to totally heal me of losing your brothers.

He asked me; "seriously...do you want me to take that?!" I sniffled out a "–no, actually." Like He didn't already know but He is a gentleman and never pushes himself. "Not all of it," I told God. "Okay, how much do you want me to take?" "Like 90 percent. Leave me something of them–I don't have a lot until I get to heaven." Done. Now my water breaks through my eyes once in a while and that's okay. It beats the nothing.

Therapists call it disassociating when you zone out to survive a pained experience, but I am determined to ditch the victim mentality. Maybe it is numbness that looks at your picture and looks away unchanged, balanced out by days when the tears just pour from a minor mishap.

Us musicians are a totally different breed of human, lol. We bond like drunks and schedule like clowns. Today, I booked a recording of a 12 song Christmas album I am planning on making this summer.

It will feel weird playing carols in August but oh well. Exciting stuff!

I miss you lots but I accept how things are now are how they have to be for a time.

Love, Mom

_____

_____

_____

"I am self-employed so if you see me talking to myself I am actually in a staff meeting."—Unknown

March 13th, 2020

Dear Riley;

Today I cleaned the Accordion house, as I call it. It just goes on forever, with umpteen bathrooms. By the time I am done I am quite sick of it.

If I was a superstitious person I would have said this really was Friday the 13th. Tripped on my own ideas.

So now the father of the psycho I am radically attracted to is acting up because he thinks I dumped his son. Well with the male chauvinistic attitude of the family it would have to be my fault it didn't work out. Even the mother is like that. If you can't beat him you join him I guess. Local talk is that: "the ––––family is only tolerated in this community." And yet they put on such airs. Lah dee dah.

Us Germans have an arrogance issue also. I fight it like crazy but sometimes I hear it from myself. Arrrgh. Lol.

This covid has everything turned hurkey murkey. Its one more thing to worry about– correction, pray about. I pray you don't get it.

A mother never stops praying for her kids. And when your Grandma K prays— things happen. She's got it going on with God.

Love, Mom

_____

_____

_____

"Mom's Sh-- List

Don't break any sh--

do not hit people with sh--

don't act like a little sh--

DO NOT FIGHT OVER SH--

don't touch other people's sh--

but most importantly

DON'T MAKE ME LOSE MY SH--"

—Unknown

March 14, 2020

Dear Riley:

Without a doubt this quote will offend some long-faced legalist but I have it on good authority— a.k.a my opinion, that being a true christian isn't about how well you judge others as wrong. Tell that to the town of H. Or any small town with a church on every block.

There's a joke about two churches across the intersection from each other and one summer morning the one congregation started singing; "Will There Be Any Stars in My Crown?" and the one across the street sang: "No, No, Not One."

I was often losing my sh-- when I raised you. You were always pushing the envelope. What I said back there... about my owning the way you were brought up, I meant it. It doesn't change that you were always leaning on my last nerve with a rusty fork...

Check out this Bible verse about dysfunctional parenting: "Can a mother forget the baby at her breast and have no compassion on the child she has borne? Though she may forget, I will not forget you! See, I have engraved you on the palms of my hands; your walls are ever before me. Your sons hasten back, and those who laid you waste depart from you." Isaiah 49: 15 (NIV)

See? Big Daddy has a tattoo of you.

I wish I had hugged you more, more often. Now I can't but I can ask God to give you a hug from me. And believe me I do.

Love, Mom

_____

_____

_____

"For the Son of Man also came not to be served, and to give his life as a ransom for many." Mark 10:45 (NLT).

March 15th, 2020

Dear Riley;

Before I even knew I was pregnant and actually thought I couldn't have children, I promised your dad I would teach our son or daughter to be proud of their heritage. Proud, not blatantly arrogant and self-deluded as a result of an over-zealous school counsellor feeding you full of sh--.

Oh God, please deliver my daughter of evil and myself of hatred, bitterness and unforgiveness. I have treated you like my servant too many times Lord, demanding things of you when you have already more than served me. Forgive me Lord, help me to serve you. Help me to forgive and keep forgiving. Amen.

Before Satan was Satan he was Lucifer, a beautiful angel in charge of all the music in heaven until he got arrogant. Pride got him kicked out from his position of Most Handsome Angel in Charge of Music and demoted to the Devil in Charge of Evil on Earth. Pride is a serious thing with God.

When we lived in the Lake the baseball caps and pickup trucks owned by natives were printed with the slogan: "Native Pride." I drove a white Cavalier so I wrote "White Pride," on the back and it got me waaay too much attention. Earned me a nickname for a while and yeah— you guessed it. I get tired of the attitude of; "there's only one culture that matters." Hello? There is room on the planet for us all or we wouldn't be here.

Soon I have to drive a friend to an evening church service. Guess you could say I have penchant for penalty.

An elder of the church I left sneered at me the other day; "you keep leaving the church." I said, "no, I have left, and my faith is still in God not any building." Instantly I was back in memory of my parents leaving the congregation my grandparents led and my Grandmother accusing my father; "you have left God." He practically yelled at the woman who practically controlled him; "The Church is not God!"

Well what can you do—I will tell you what you cannot do— hold people against God. God is still good all the time and God is good in spite of me.

Love, Mom

_____

_____

_____

"He makes all things new." Revelation 21:5 (NIV, paraphrased).

March 16, 2020

Dear Riley;

I pray you and Rachel are restored to all God created you to be despite my mistakes in parenting. Oh, I would throw myself in front of a train if it benefited either of you, for what it is worth.

I told you once that the church (or some of them) function like the whore in Revelation and the one I just extracted myself from is a tossup between cult and whore. Get everyone in here praying. No wonder they don't want to address the rich man who flat out harassed me three Sundays in a row. They want his money and the joke is on them...he doesn't even pay a full tithe. He donates very little. I guess they are hoping and he is joking. Amen.

Anyway, I always felt supremely judged there and the real anger I have is toward myself for not getting out sooner. A good looking single female in a church will be punished because she is a threat to mousy married women and bored married men. (Not that I am attracted to myself but I do shine up nice.) A single male will be ass-kissed. Here we went again. Man I hate that! No pun intended.

You know my love life always did read like a white man's fishing licence on restricted waters...catch and release only. Now I am middle aged and I cannot believe the domestic abusers I have known and the good men I have not. So I pray for a revolution among men...

The corona virus is already aggravating me... the government in my opinion has responded opportunistically with panic-spread: "look at us keeping you all safe and giving you money to survive... aren't we great?!" We have never shut the globe down for ANYTHING else that killed people. Just saying.

My opinions usually get me into trouble so I should be careful when and where I voice them. One day. One day.

Love, Mom

"Let God fight your battles. He hasn't lost one yet."–Unknown

March 17th, 2020

Dear Riley;

Today I decided to just live by heaven's economy and rely of God to supply what I needed instead of stressing out.

I remember how you used to dream of going to Disneyland. There was no money for it, but I still wish we could go one day– the three of us. Your step grandmother at the time suggested going to the West Edmonton Mall, a.k.a Canadian Disneyland. But again...funding issues.

Do you remember how I paid for guitar/voice/piano lessons for you and Rachel and I haven't got one musician out of the bunch, lol.

Sometimes I am afraid for you when I think of the venom you have so freely poured out with zero ownership for your actions. Oh I know we are all capable of it and you are your mother's daughter; but my conscience bothers me if I do wrong and you don't seem to have one, so I worry, fret, and then pray. In that order. One day I hope to shortcut to prayer. And praise.

Prayer changes things–praise keeps what prayer has changed.

There is a "Riley-Drawer," in my dresser now where I toss a gift or card for you into every now and then. It will replace this journal probably.

I would cover these walls with your artwork if I had access to it through you. Only then. You have your father's gift.

It's time to get busy for the day again. Busyness helps, but I think it is also a drug too many of us are trying to numb our pain with. The trouble is you get rid of pain by feeling it, not running from it.

Love, Mom

_____

_____

_____

"You cannot learn what you already think you know."–

Tim Han

March 18th, 2020

Dear Riley;

In the story of the prodigal son, it says: "the father saw him coming from afar." And we "parents of prodigals are to do the same. Sometimes I do, sometimes I don't.

Since when is my faith perfect...the word also says He keeps us in perfect faith. God believes in us–why else would he have faith? He is God. Doesn't that just blow your mind?!

Today is a blah, down kind of day again. Your Gramma K says: "It's a good thing not everyday is the same." She also says; "No is an answer too." She is plucky.

In your educational travels, did you ever come across

"Resignation Syndrome." Where people have given up and all they do is sleep. Children get it in a hostage situation as a means of coping, but I have seen it in adults.

I can't wait to tease you about all your; "fancy book learnin'." Lol.

Some days, today being a prime example thereof; it feels like I have been assigned to push a boulder up a mountain with my nose minus the aid of machinery, or even pulleys. The mountain has been there for a long time, perhaps forever. I don't remember a season of life without it. No pun intended, but its been a long haul.

You were raised in such poverty, there were times we didn't have a car, phone, or even a vacuum cleaner. We lived on food banks. People treated us like less than. We already had less than. But the last two paragraphs are victim mode, and I need to reframe. I am grateful for all Big Daddy has brought me through. Thanks to my life experiences, I can relate to a vast amount of people and empathize with them, and that is never a waste or time. "Through many dangers, toils and snares I have already come." Amen and hallelujah!

Love, Mom

_____

_____

_____

"When you don't wait on the Lord, you give the enemy an opportunity to give you counterfeits." —Unknown

March 19th, 2020

Dear Riley;

It has become an eerie world of empty stores and paranoid service providers. All a panic, yet when a masked man (or woman) enters the building that is now normal. Negativity sells better than positivism. I FEEL that the government is using this pandemic to sell themselves: "we care so much about your safety. We want to keep you safe." Sorry no sale.

The world is wrapping up for a grand finale and I say lets have it. Beam me up.

Peace has come today. I just want to be the just who lives by faith, the sheep who hears His voice and the righteous who doesn't have to beg bread. Tranquility, I am learning from God— is not a passive experience. The word says to seek peace and pursue it. We have a part to play. Once again— the contrast between being a victim or an action figure.

I pray you will be delivered of and protected from evil. The devil has no chance against a mother's prayers. Do you remember good old G, the mother of the church we used to attend— she would always say; "Satan is a defeated foe but he is also a jerk."

Last night I dreamt about you and Rachel as little girls. Well-you will always be my little girls. A mother can always see her baby when she looks at her child, you would think. Unless she is too messed up.

Do you remember the empty apartment we started out with when I moved us to Alberta? We found an old karaoke machine and went through a Rick Trevino/ Patty Loveless/ Tracy Byrd phase of listening to and singing: "Out of Control Raging Fire," and "Holding Heaven." We slept on the floor on swimming inflatables.

Life in H is turning into the same life as life in La Crete, and I never wanted to return to my hometown of judgment passing and gossip robbing one of any privacy even if inaccurate. Its enough to turn anyone of lesser faith into a water tower sniper. Kidding. You just ignore it after a while. Let'em talk...cuz if they are talking about me they are leaving everyone else alone. I am about to charge for that service though. Haha. On Instagram there was a quote; "they have to talk about you...cuz if they talk about themselves no one would listen."

I told your Grammy K I was tempted to spread a baloney rumour about my rich Grandfather having passed and leaving me millions and then watch the false friendships come rolling in. She, the ever wise one, said not to, that could just cause trouble with Revenue Canada.

These are days of great contemplation. Mid life crisis perhaps, because I want to cut my hair into a Mohawk, am wondering what to do with the rest of my life and planning to buy a motorcycle. Yikes.

Love, Mom

_____

_____

_____

"If you're praying about it, God's working on it."—Unknown

"Prayer changes things— praise keeps what prayer has changed."—Unknown

March 20th, 2020

Dear Riley;

I finally brought up something to your sister the other day that I had observed for a long time. Being the product of a split does something to you and the way it manifests in her is she cannot handle a gift from me sitting on the same shelf as a present from her dad. Literally they cannot be on the same shelf because we were never on the same page. You both have an issue with supporting or appreciating both parents at the same time. I recall your tirade about how "dad-was-wonderful-you-sucked-supremely." We are all a mixture of good and evil, pillars in the community are sometimes just piles of baloney and the sanest members of society can be the biggest nuts going and the mentally ill are sometimes the kindest, sanest people you will ever meet. That all being said—if you are old enough to drive you are old enough to get in your car and drive to a therapists office and get help. If you're teachable you're fixable.

I pray the word over this situation with you; Lord, go before me and make the crooked paths straight: break in pieces the gates of brass, and cut in sunder the bars of iron. Isaiah 45:2 (KJV)

I believe the word also in Isaiah 54:15: "If anyone fiercely attacks you it will not be from Me. Whoever attacks you will fall because of you." (NASB). Amen.

After everything that has happened, I am becoming rather impervious to personal assaults. I mean I avoid them because I do not want to be triggered into a PTSD blackout and wake up wringing someone's neck, but do they devastate me, no. Plus I find physical exercise helps channel unexpressed anger.

Why am I telling you these things— because you are a lot like me; our mantra is "first take no crap." Lol.

When you and your sister both acted up at the same time, it felt like a proverbial black SUV had pulled up in front of our house, pulled you in, slammed the door and drove off. I felt helpless, standing there on the proverbial sidewalk without a phone call. Yet God says I can call on him anytime. Duh. So I do.

Love, Mom

"Worry does no empty tomorrow of it's sorrow, it empties today of its strength." –Corrie Ten Boom

March 21, 2020

Dear Riley;

Now the churches are shut down too because of the virus scare. I just want life to return to normal already without the added struggle. There is so much sickness and disease for which nothing was shut down or interrupted. Our government loves drama like a toxic individual does.

Church continues to be a household word, most are still geared for people that are married with children, and the problem with that theory is there are more people like me than there are people like them. So get with the program I say. It is an outdated system for spirituality and heavily in crisis I'd say, even without covid. I mean, the kingdom of God is current but it does not operate like some people are better than others. The base of the cross is an equal playing field. Everyone from Ted Bundy to Mother Teresa and in between could receive the same amount of grace, mercy, and forgiveness of sins.

Oh for some ambition. Suddenly time has opened up and there is not enough structure to get everything done. Isn't that weird how that works.

Anyway, I miss you lots. I pray our relationship gets a giant reset. Amen.

Love, Mom

_____

_____

_____

Nothing is impossible, the word itself spells: "I am possible."—Unknown

March 27th, 2020

Dear Riley;

I still confuse your handle with the Lord's because I keep a Riley journal and a prayer journal. Feeling flattered yet?

What is it when a Mom calls someone by everyone else's name first? Even the dogs name gets in there...Johnny/Suzy/Markus-Bingo! Go clean your room! Lol.

Man this town is stuck in the past. People having babies past their prime. I say 35 is the cutoff for both genders, because even the men don't have the same energy level that they once did. But around here we have a make-your-own-grandchild program. I know a girl-tall and gangly -could hunt geese with a rake- her parents had her at 42 and she is riddled with mental health issues and developmental delays. The worst thing yet is when she discovered the difference between boys and girls and never recovered from it if ya know what I mean. Now I am being the judgmental one. And having lived the life...but it disgusts me now.

The boy next door is a relative of the author Janette Oake and he reminds me of Josh from one of her books. I grew up with my nose in her books and now I am pestering to meet her.

The boys in this town—there are about a dozen or so 30 to 45 year old virgins that never outgrew the "girls are yucky," stage. Anywhere else in the real world… kids are having sex as young as 9. What am I doing surrounded by all these puritans? Lol. As if they don't all handle it themselves with the five finger discount. Ahem!

My prayer for you today is that you will come to a place where you see yourself through God's eyes. It's where truth and mercy get married. Amen.

Love, Mom

_____

_____

_____

"Don't piss on my neck and tell me it's raining."
-Unknown

March 23rd, 2020

Dear Riley;

There sure aren't people balanced with people in this rinky-dink town, it's very disproportionate. There are not ten single gals for ten single cowboys...not that I would want to play cowboys and idiots. Cowboys tend to cheat hence my heroes have always killed cowboys, lol.

I have learned that people do what they do because of who they are not because of who I am. Cheaters, liars, thieves.

Let me beguile you with the tale of being on something dot dating site from hell. The men are spewing things on their profiles like; "you better show up on our first date with a spreadsheet from your successful business showing a profit margin and you better have a lucrative career and your own assets, have an active credit card and pick up half the tab or we are done talking." I told my friend about it and she said; "oh. They're the b-----es now." Lol.

In my life the guys with a gap in their front teeth are ALWAYS abusive clowns. I had one date lined up and then the guy messaged me; "oh forget the restuarant-just come to my house at blah dee dah address." I blocked him turned around and went home.

Lord love a duck (senior swear) the stunts they are pulling. May as well call it jerks.com. Well? I call things as they are.

Sometimes they say—oh hi, I like you but you live two hours away. Awe...whatsa matter? Mommy can't drive you?! Sarcasm. I guess at this stage in life we all have baggage, I don't deny mine.

One guy said; "I think you women all just want a free meal ticket." I replied, "I think you men all just want a free sex ticket." And they use the word "love," to get it. I hate the word love.

One guy just wanted me to send "sexy pics," for you-know-what reason. It's like having a real woman is out dated and self-um, satisfaction is the thing now. But of course they say that about us too, "men were replaced when batteries were invented."

If it wasn't all just geared about money. I get that two people have to have complete lives in order to have a third thing together. I get that two halves make a quarter when two empty souls try to meet. I had to let go of the 50's life I signed on for, which was easy once I realized I could never be the yes wife nor could I hold up my end of the bargain with babies. If I got

pregnant now I'd shoot myself. Granted I'd miss but...
shoot myself I would. No offence. Lol.

Anyway, I am a hopeless romantic and I say if and
when two people right for each other meet they will
figure out an equation for being together that works
for both.

Love, Mom

_____

_____

_____

"You don't have to be approved by man if you have been appointed by God." —Unknown

March 24th, 2020

Dear Riley;

And time hangs heavy on our hands as the world shuts down over the virus. It used to be you could fart and clear a room, now you clear your throat and the room empties. I do not do well with time on my hands, I need the busy drug like most people seem to...and one seems to have time or money not both.

Today I published a book on Amazon, the first one of the trilogy. Woo hoo. This journal will one day be published also.

Your sister is moving in with her boyfriend soon. I haven't met him in person, only by phone thanks to her workaholism and priorities. I am proud of how you girls can hold down multiple jobs and save money the way you do. You got the work ethic from me...the rest is a puzzle.

Hopefully publishing books is a real game changer, but we'll see. Wouldn't it be nice to get out of poverty and lack and being the working class poor? Beam me up already! I have to pray believing it isn't going to happen. I mean I don't endorse the New Age "think-myself-into-a-new-sports-car," mode of thinking but the Book-Inspired-By-Love-Eruptions (Bible) says: "let him ask in faith, nothing wavering." James 1:6-8 (NIV) "But when he asks, he must believe and not doubt, because he who doubts is like a wave tossed by the sea, blown and tossed by the wind. That man should not think he will receive anything from the Lord; he is double minded man unstable in all he does." My argument before the Lord is: "but nothing happens when I am believing..."

I hope you are well and healthy.

Love, Mom

_____

_____

_____

"I can never understand which is more painful the lies I believed or the truths I did not."–Unknown

March 25th, 2020

Dear Riley;

I wonder what you are doing right now, besides socially isolating. Will this thing ever end? Of course it will-

once the government gets the power, publicity, and prestige they want out of it. Then, and only then, miraculously, they will find a vaccine that will get all the glory.

I cope by burying myself in music, music makes it all okay, lol.

"God didn't bring me this far to bring me this far," someone said in a church circle not long ago. Is it wisdom or do you find yourself waiting for the next line? I can almost hear you laughing at it.

How will life be when we talk again? I wonder sometimes. I am trying to picture it. One day, kid. One day.

This town continues to be holier than now. Oh well, Less pressure to perform on me, more for them. Or I am not in the right circle. The unbelievers seem to be the friendly, accepting, non-judgmental ones. Sometimes I argue that before God: "why would I want someone else to become a christian just to enlarge the jerk population?" It seems they are the worst ones for transgressions, they fall all over themselves to get someone else "saved," and the biggest problems to contend with are the song leaders, the pious peeps that are still married to their first date, etc. Sheep bite, someone once told me. Well maybe if the vet removed the stick outta their butts they wouldn't...grrrrr. But one shouldn't hold people against God.

I have taken to wearing wigs and I make no big effort to hide the fact. Nothing to hide and hiding nothing. The poofy 80's one was a bit much. Plus I don't have the corresponding parts, ha ha. Dolly Parton once said; "it takes a lot of money to make me look this cheap."

Well I have to go super glue my fingertips together so that the cracks can heal and they quit bleeding... heaven forbid I would ever wear gloves to clean.

Love, Mom

"The only job where you start at the top is digging a hole."—Unknown

March 26th, 2020

Dear Riley;

I am trying so hard to keep my life surrendered to God and have all the channels open between He and I. It's the only way. Gramma K always said: "if you want God's help, keep it holy."

And although my spirit was always designed to be at one with its creator, I have ulterior motives; I want God to bring you back to himself and our little family.

You were always someone who took things very personally, and its hard to take it any other way when it personally affects us. It helps to understand that sin is actually against God. When we do wrong, we don't sin against people nor do they sin against us. Sin is against God— why else would he "reward every man according to how he has done," (Romans 2:6) if it was none of His business? Right? The Bible says: "The Lord will fight for you, you need only keep still."

Today your sister and I got into a tiff over religious differences. She said defiantly, not for the first time,

that she is into science not spirituality. I said, well great, there is a christian science centre not far from the place we used to live in R. That shut her up good, after one little: "ok." See, it isn't all a cakewalk through the tulip park with Rachel and I either. If she expected an argument there wasn't one.

Someone told me that mothers are crucified by their daughters and sons hate their fathers, but the dynamics crisscross to where mothers are favoured by their sons and fathers by daughters. Have sons Riley. Just kidding. Have both, but when the time is right. As if it is all in our hands right? NOT.

Love, Mom

"Investing in yourself is the best thing you can do."
-Warren Buffet

March 27th, 2020

Dear Riley;

It has been a nearly a year since I moved here with him. We finally parted ways after 6 years of on again off again financial abuse. The man loved work— he could watch me do it all day. I did everything alone, so why have a man?!

After a year, I thing Angelo has pooed on every front lawn and back alley there is in this town. Most people here are friendly, they chat you up without an introduction.

When I made my mistakes in life most of them were men. Shortly afterwards of moving here, where a different ex originates from, he heard about it and came pounding on my door like an entitled ass and I didn't answer the door. That has kind of been the policy for safety anyway— that if I am not expecting you I won't answer. That and there being nothing attractive about a man who acts like you are his property. Its partnership not ownership, in a healthy relationship. Which we were not.

This house would delight you, so unique and quaint and full of nooks and crannies. A secret passageway to the bathroom...right? Someone was thinking. If ever under siege, one can still go pee. Hee hee.

Living alone has its challenges. I told God if he wants me to have roommates he will have to send them, because they would very much have to be the right people and I only get tire kickers over the internet. So once in a while the silence is deafening in between the dogs dedication to guarding the yard and almost incessant barking.

Pets help with loneliness, but they are not the be all end all. There is still something missing where my chillins should be. I feel like Tom Hank on Castaway sometimes. Lol.

They will milk this social isolation thing until we are all talking to a smiley sticker on an empty gas can. Yikes.

Well, I always did say; "it's driving me crazy but it won't be a long trip," lol.

And hey let's face it, sanity is for losers.

Love, Mom

_____

_____

_____

"God never wastes pain."–Rick Warren

"The pain you've been feeling can't compare to the joy that's coming." Romans 8:18 (Paraphrased).

March 28th, 2020

Dear Riley;

I remember the first time you had something like a bipolar episode, running away when I tried to pick you up from school. You were all of twelve, running off with friends and admitted to the youth shelter for the first time of many. At one point you were driven over to the basement suite we lived in to pick up some more clothing, talking a hundred clicks a minute, said you had been staying with "S," and the family thereof. I had no idea if S was a boy or a girl and couldn't get the answer either. I could barely recognize you except your physical colouring. Your entire demeanour and complexion had changed. But anyway, you stopped your prattling, looked at me with big, flat, empty eyes and asked: "what's happening to me?" And without answers, I said: "I don't know." I knew you fell under the influence of an over-zealous school counsellor determined to make her career out of the stories she fed you and it practically destroyed you.

Public school is one of the times where I lost you. But not forever.

What I believe is you had some kind of mental collapse or breakdown. You told me a few years ago: "I don't want there to be something wrong with me." Well, the truth is, we all have something wrong with us, and if we think we don't, that's our "something wrong," talking.

You can help more people when you have been there and done that than if you have lived a sheltered life. And the truth is, the mind is just one more part on the human body that can get overloaded and sick and it, like the rest of the body, can be healed also.

Mental health joke:

"Roses are red

violets are blue

I'm a schizophrenic

and so am I."

What did one shrink say to the other?

"You're fine, how am I?"

"I used to be schizophrenic but we're okay now!" That one's a total misnomer. Multiple personality disorder is not the same as schizophrenia.

Well anyway, I hope you get the help you need. And the healing. Some angels have clipped wings.

Love, Mom

_____

_____

_____

"Some days I am more wolf than woman and I am still learning how to stop apologizing for my wild." –Unknown

"Don't let other people tell you who you are." –Unknown

March 29th, 2020

Dear Riley;

Do you remember the Japanese phase you went through? I loved helping you gather the oriental artifacts so much I kept it up for a while after the phase was over. It was hilarious the day you came home from school frustrated with bullies and declared yourself an oriental. Lol. Like it was that simple. Even now if I catch myself dropping a word around other people I say; "oh pardon my Gerpanese."

My social life, which has always been the equivalent of house arrest, now has to be that way. Which changes everything. Funny how lack of choice alters the same scene. We are back to a 1930s chicken-pox quarantine. With all the technology, medical research and knowledge, we are still nowhere. Or so it seems.

I don't believe anyone or anything is beyond God's reach. My prayers for you today are to be delivered of evil, I feel led to ask for deliverance of demonic possession. I plead the blood flood of Jesus over your life for deliverance, salvation and redemption. Amen Lord.

Hell hath no torment like an anguished mother's prayers. Nope.

I pray also Father God, that she would grow a conscience over all her dealings, give her a heart of flesh rather than a heart of stone. I beg the merits of the cross be applied to Riley's life for salvation. I pray for protection of her deeds until such time. May every curse be blocked and returned, may the mouth of a liar be stopped just as your word says. Please heal my family—the language of faith is not please but thank you—so thank you that you have heard my pleas for my family. In Jesus Name, Amen.

I sleep a lot when I am processing loss, and I don't mean to walk or lay around in lack of faith. I don't think that's what it is. When you sleep you don't hurt. And when you sleep you dream...and sometimes the people you miss show up. Hence sleep is my bestie.

When you were two and pestering me when I was pregnant with Rachel, I finally begged; "will you please go play while Mommy finishes whatever-I-was-doing? Pretty please with sugar on top?" So up the cupboard you went and right for the sugar bowl." I said (in exasperation) "Now what are you doing?" "I'm getting you some sugar," you replied. Only you left out the silent h. Haha.

Love, Mom

"God knows how to give you back what the enemy convinced you that you lost."–Unknown

March 30, 2020

Dear Riley;

Well the quarantine has affected book publication, I can only upload to kindle because there is no one on duty at the paper production end. Oh well. I would say the biggest loss would be not getting started at all.

Today I am clinging to gratitude. It is a powerful antidote to victim hood, weak faith, and addiction. I am grateful for what God has brought me through and what He is bringing me to.

When your Great Grandpa K was informed my Grandmother had passed he said: "oh thank God," and people snicker when I say that before they hear the end of the story. He believed what the word said; "in everything give thanks." Then he wept openly and out loud at her funeral, a big Mennonite no-no. A display of emotions was worldly and unnecessary.

I found my grandfather's Conscientious Objectors Camp registration online once and I kick myself for not printing it. Now I have to pay someone to locate it for me.

Life is on hold now but many are catching up on the things we need to, like family time and projects long overdue.

Angelo has to go to the vet this week. I know now where the saying comes from; "sicker than a dog." He has been my best friend with chronic ear infections and cost, and when his time is up I am not sure I am doing this again.

I wonder what last name you go by. Perhaps your fathers or grandmothers; J----- or F-------.

It's bedtime, so I'll say goodnight.

Love, Mom

_____

_____

_____

"It's one thing to lose the people you love. It is another to lose yourself. That is a greater loss." —Unknown

March 37th, 2020

Dear Riley;

Do you know how much money is enough? Just one dollar more. Isn't that the truth. It doesn't actually satisfy, it keeps you running. I have been accused by the man who tried to live off of me that I only care about money, and that allegedly "all you need is love." I said "well? Ever try to pay a grocer with love? You'll get arrested." Me tooed. I mean, you can't get far without money, even the homeless need it for their next cup of coffee or cellphone expenses.

For you first two years, it was just you and I. We did everything together, sleep, bathe, you name it. I wonder now if it was my biggest mistake.

When you first hold your your newborn baby, you never think it will come to this; stonewalling and estrangement. But when you have kids you do the best you can and they grow up and make their choices.

Today I prayed for you; seizing the demons over your life and paralyzing them in the name of Jesus so they lose their grip. You see, the devil walks around like a roaring lion but Jesus IS the lion of Judah. Amen! Hallelujah!

People reading this might think I am nuts but that is okay. What they think of me is none of my business and lets keep it that way. If we all knew exactly what the other person thought none of us would be friends.

During the phase of my life around the suicide attempt I discovered two things; that the cruelty of the public school playground doesn't change it just shifts to adulthood, and there are the usual North-ends-of-south-bound-cows and there are genuine caring people that would shed tears over the pain of a total stranger like it was their own. I will never forget Dr. M the male resident doctor nor Dr. H., nor the staff at the Psych Hospital.

I have felt so judged as single woman in a religious town-censored-and then judged even harsher after the suicide attempt and hospitalization. What can I say-it has been a celebrity lifestyle without the riches- all fame and no fortune but I am praying about that too. When we really and truly get who and how God is, when we look at others all we give is love.

Love, Mom

_____

_____

_____

"There is no shortcut to anyplace worth going."– Beverly Sills

"My dreams are bigger than my imperfections."– Cecilia Berkley

April 1st, 2020

Dear Riley;

"It is easier to ask forgiveness than permission," said someone. Easier for who? The culprit, obviously, not so much the recipient of the behaviour.

Are you keeping yourself going with your art-sales, I wonder.

I had to leave a job today because I cleared my throat as I always do and it equalled the corona virus, of course. I have evidently had it my entire life because I have always cleared my throat. People are getting ridiculous. And since when is social snottiness a virus preventative?! Arrrgh.

Angelo had to go to the vet today with another ear infection. I just want to marry a vet already, ha ha.

These days I have been partying with God; cranking the music that mentions him and talking to the Almighty a lot more than usual. There is silver lining to covid 19. Not much– I'd hate to try and live on it, but some blessings have come of it.

God and I also talk as I walk Angie, maybe people think thats crazy and I still do not care. Sanity is for losers and normal is over-rated.

Love, Mom

_____

_____

_____

"I will take sickness away from the midst of you."
Exodus 23:25 (NKJV).

April 2, 2020

Dear Riley:

You were pow wow dancing in the womb. I realize that
now, stretching and leaping as far as my internal
organs would allow you to, ha ha.

Today I prayed the dirty thirties quarantine
will be over and life will go back to normal, maybe.
What does normal even mean anymore—in AA they
say normal; is just a setting on your bread maker.
One has to be grateful to be "cooking" at all in these
sketchy times.

I have often wondered without really wanting to know;
what hurts the worst, losing a kid to death or rebellion.
Technically with the miscarriages I do know, but I
mean raising a kid and they die or they rebel. There
are days I wonder while silently screaming so I drown
out any possible answer. I don't want to know. Pain is
pain and I don't want any more.

We were Olympic-championship broke on your sixteenth
birthday and I tried to do what I could, but you
didn't hide your disappointment and it went the way
of another argument. So we have to do your sixteenth
one day for real. Remember, no one can cheat you out

of what God wants you to have. Not even a 16th b-day party when you are 30. Ha ha.

Love, Mom

_____

_____

_____

"The Lord is my rock, my fortress, and my deliverer, my God, my mountain where I seek refuge; my shield and the horn of my salvation, my stronghold." Psalm 18:2 (HCSB).

April 3rd, 2020

Dear Riley,

Today is one of those days where it feels as if I have made zero progress in this healing journey. The way you intermittently bond with Rachel and then pull the moat up if she doesn't ditch me also is out and out emotional blackmail if not abuse. You have not just been disrespectful and rude, I believe you act in a cruel, manipulative, malicious, vindictive and downright venomous way. I see everything you do as an outlet for the insatiable revenge you seek against me for having been a reactive parent who swatted your behind. It worries me that you seem to think that as long as you function from a victim stance your behaviours toward others that you view as perpetrators are justified. I believe making amends sometimes means letting someone know how their behaviour affected you minus the bitterness, the anger, and unforgivness. And the truth is, you have been part of the reason I wished I was dead and couldn't hurt anymore. You didn't make my choices for me—never have nor will. No one did. But someday soon, I pray you see the affects of your actions on other people. That is my point.

Oh I know I wanted to raise two kids that could survive in this brutal world; I wanted to raise two girls that would not take anybody's crap but you have so far surpassed it that I live my life waiting for a certain phone call.

I am not doing well at social isolation, stuck in my house, in my head with these thoughts and memories. Don't leave me unsupervised with my mind!

Every day is a new adventure with corona-not-beer. Today I saw the department of motor vehicles was closed over it. People are not even returning phone calls or emails. How do you catch the virus off of a wireless device, pray tell?!

So far, our little town does not have any cases of covid-19, maybe because we are behind the times, lol.

It is a pet peeve of mine that people in H seem to be so big on breeding past their prime. A local girl I know-so tall she's always close to the Lord-literally-and can hunt eagles with a mere reach-was conceived by a pair of 42 year olds. Now they are 85 and cannot relax in retirement years because their phone is always ringing and its their menopause baby: "the power is out can I still flush the toilet?" Igh carumba!

Your uncle-my only brother, was had when my parents were 39 and 42 and he is a walking bundle of health problems. I get right irate when people don't seem to even consider that men get too old to have babies. My opinion is the law after all-kidding!

I wish I had bottled your laughter and carried it with me. When you have the giggles it sounds like music. On a day like this I need that melody.

Now the one lah-dee-dah church is opening their doors for prayer on Sunday morning like a mosque. One slight problem...we are not Muslims? There are none here? And we can pray anywhere? Duh.

"It is important that a man is romantic and brings you flowers. It is also important that a man makes you laugh, provides, and is affectionate. It is equally important that these four men don't find out about each other" (Author unknown). Lol!

Well, on that cheery note...bye.

Love, Mom

"I will give you a new heart and put a new spirit in you; I will remove from you your heart of stone and give you a heart of flesh." Ezekiel 36:26 (KJV).

April 4th, 2020

Dear Riley;

I pray God will change your heart like His word says, and that He will be with you during this time. All the time, but especially now during global down time. Please make it all be over soon Lord!

Father God, I pray for forgiveness of wrong attitudes and thoughts—anything that would hinder my prayers from being answered for Riley. Deliver her from evil and its deception of rightness, transform her into a mighty warrior for you. Amen!

I used to call you Ri-LEH. It sounded aboriginal. I miss those days.

If God didn't "bottle my tears," like scriptures says in Psalm 56:8, where would any of us hurting Moms be. "You keep track of all my sorrows. You have collected all my tears in your bottle. You have recorded each one in your book."(NLT).

Amen. Love, Mom

_____

_____

_____

"When we accept our limits we can rise above them."
-Unknown

April 5th, 2020

Dear Riley;

Some days I feel like telling the sun not to shine. But wounds still need light if they are going to be treated.

Will you go to school for the rest of your life, I wonder. With the status card paying for everything, you could become a professional student I suppose. I have misgivings about whether or not I did the right thing helping you get Indian status. And yes, it is still called that, the department of INDIAN Affairs granted the card and no one ever sent their children out to play "cowboys and first nations."

I hope by the time you have any power as a social worker— you probably do now, but I hope none over my disability file. Until God delivers you.

Sometimes I watch shows that have a lot of Aboriginal culture content so I can feel close to you. Other times I cannot stand it. There is a certain agitation that goes with grief and trauma and I don't mean wash cycle.

Friends and acquaintances that have lost a child to physical death or know of someone who has argue with me that at least you can come back after you turn around. I argue that with a passing-yes-the pain is greater and feels more final. But it is one big wham and then it lessens unless it morphs into complicated grief.

The couple near here that lost all three daughters to a farming accident some years ago had said at one point they wished them back—even if the girls were rebellious.

But their daughters never told them to die a slow painful death and that they wouldn't even acknowledge them at the funeral or even help provide one, but rather throw their own mother's body into a ditch for the wild animals to devour.

It helps to remember you are sick with what looks like some form of bipolar illness. There are a few. Your dad was diagnosed in prison with Schizophrenia, but he argued the shrink just didn't like him and he had been fresh out of solitary confinement.

Love, Mom

"There is no shortcut to anyplace worth going."
—Unknown.

April 6th, 2020

Dear Riley;

Today, I continue to feel like the world is grey. The Bible talks about shining light into the darkness and how when we walk with Christ we are not stuck in the dark like it's a locked closet. My writing desk is in the attic and some days the staircase seems longer than others. Someone once said; "everyone wants to have written, no one wants to write."

I thought writing about my adult life would be easier as far as memory goes. Hah. Was I hoping or joking?!

Life in quarantine is surreal, yet real enough to wonder how much longer? Are we there yet? No doubt it will perturb some people off when I say I believe this pandemic will be over when the government has milked it for what power, prestige, and self-promotion it can get out of it...but then I cringe over how cancer and other disease research never results in a cure because they want to keep the donations coming. You would think though, that this virus is only costing them money...so why not seek a quick end?!

It's hard to watch you live your entire life like a train wreck. Not that I have access to your life, but when you lure Rachel into a relationship and then

demand she ditch me or else you are done with her...
wow. That is hard to take.

I pray constantly, but often it's like the line from
the Alan Jackson country song: "Monday Morning
Church;"

"I can't seem to talk to God without yelling anymore."
Well, He who has transformed my complaints into
intercessory prayer can surely convert my yelling
into the cries of His children He promises to hear.

Love, Mom

_____

_____

_____

"You either overcome your demons or you waste energy trying to keep them concealed." -Me, paraphrased from an Instagram quote.

April 7th, 2020

Dear Riley;

Your sister tells me-when you have contact, that you are not even going to therapy. And from the eighty trillion hate emails I received when I had the former email account including one where you attempted to put a curse on me; I gather your spirituality is in a dark place.

The Seventh Day Adventists always said; "Let's get on our knees and really get God's attention." Oh trust me-I have been wearing out the floorboards of this old shanty. But I don't think it gets God's attention-it helps us focus more on our prayers, like journaling them.

My request of God is that He will bring you to a place where you see yourself through His eyes.

It must be hard to lose your Dad twice-he wasn't part of our lives to begin with until you were eleven and then it was drunk phone calls for three years, then you met him and knew him for a brief few years before he passed away at age 54. I am guessing of Pneumonia. He reminded me a little of Guy Penrod, a scrawnier, more scarred version but still.

I wonder how far bitterness, anger and unforgiveness will take you. And for you to still be demanding an apology from me after everything...that tells me you are addicted to this thing—when you do not see your part and only see a victim in the bathroom mirror, that is the toxic stance of an addict. Alcohol and drugs get a lot of glory but addiction can be anything. Well—those two used to get a lot of glory before Rick Warren created Celebrate Recovery. I took you there once along with your dangerous boyfriend.

Your dad could never bury the hatchet without leaving a map either. Once he was offended, that was it.

You cannot put a curse on me, Jesus did away with all the curses on the cross by making Himself one and then being put to death. And greater is He who is in me than he who is in the world. (My paraphrase; 1 John 4:4)

Love, Mom

"There are two mistakes one can make along the road to truth...not going all the way, and not starting."-Buddha

April 8th, 2020

Dear Riley;

I always say the truth will always set you free of the people who can't handle the truth.

Tomorrow is your grandfather's 74th birthday. You and he always got along famously. Just like in the book which you were named after. Only your relationship was largely long distance.

It bugs me that my parents were always piddle poor and broke as a joke/brokefolk and it bugs me how people with money look down on those who don't as if we are deliberately poor to irritate someone else. Then they moved and moved-sometimes 3 times a year because no place is good enough or whatever, and it costs and costs to move and they were not flipping houses either. Grandpa K should not be passing his medicals for the driving but let's face it doctors get paid out of tax dollars-my paperwork was practically filled out before I got into the room, it seemed.

It appears to be springtime out there, finally. Except the wind still cuts off your ears and hands them to you...along with your ass. Sorry, couldn't resist.

Since when does Christianity mean acting like a giant stiff?! I have just been ganged up on/given the group silent treatment by the church "leadership," over gossip. WOW. Wish I had moved here and kept to my friggen self.

I wonder how much counselling we will need to be reconciled or how God will do it.

I pray Ephesians 2:14 (NIV) over us: "For he is our peace, who hath made the two one and has destroyed the barrier, the dividing wall of hostility..."

"So also will be the word that I speak-it will not fail to do what I plan for it, it will do everything I send it to do." Isaiah 55:11 (GNB)

I am praying the word-using God's own promises against Him, so to speak.

"Not by might nor by power, but by my Spirit says the Lord Almighty." Zechariah 4:6 (NIV)

I wish I could hug you and never let go. We wouldn't even have to talk...my baby is sick, I keep reminding myself. And no matter how big a mother's babies get, she always sees them as her baby.

"He sent His word and healed them, and delivered them from their destructions." Psalm 107:20 (KJV) Oooo please Lord. I know the language of faith is not please but thank you, so I thank you that you have heard me. Thank you that you have done what I am asking for. Amen.

Love, Mom

_____

_____

_____

"Walking in God's favour does not mean you will not face adversity."–Mike Evans

April 9th, 2020

Dear Riley;

It's hard to do nothing, you never know when you are done. With all this time on my hands I would have thought all the household projects would get caught up. But no...

Every time I walk by the craft store I think of you.

I wonder if I would even be notified if you got injured or worse. Probably not, unless the law was involved. Otherwise the aboriginal culture would claim you and take it to La Loche to bury and I wouldn't argue.

Your mantra is to tell me how awful I was as a parent, yet for the behaviour I was dealing with ALONE, I think I showed amazing restraint. For how many times I wanted to throttle your ass, and did not, I think I should receive a medal.

Every deed is a seed and comes back treed. My own version of Hosea 8:7. When they sow the wind, they will reap a storm!"(GNB)

I do not believe in luck or karma, they are New Age and Eastern Religion beliefs. I believe in reaping and sowing.

Your crop is coming in girl, and it's gonna be pain fruit.

And as per usual; I WILL get that phone call, and be expected to fix it.

Will it even be possible for me to help you in that reaping mode, should I be involved with you in your suffering then or back away and let you fully take the consequences like I should have along time ago. In some ways I think I was too lax as a parent. And will that then be seen and judged as unforgiveness? I much prefer the terminology; "self-preservation."

Love, Mom

_____

_____

_____

"If we all did the things we are capable of doing, we would literally astound ourselves." Thomas Edison

April 10th, 2020

Dear Riley;

Do you remember when I fund raised for your trip to New York by busking at the smaller farmer's market in R_____? You stood beside me and plucked the paper money out of the Accordion case as fast as it landed in there. Which is what you are supposed to do; not let the money pile up because then you set yourself up to be robbed of more tips or just plain robbed. We also collected bottles, I crawled under chain link fencing to get the empties on the other side while you pouted that the bottles and cans were not coming fast enough. Your dad simply got cranky when asked to contribute anything and did nothing. Yet you say he is the better parent.

Then, when you went on the trip after I had pawned my Accordion in between gigs how many times to meet the deadlines for payments, I was inundated with texts from you about all the ailments you were experiencing. I said well don't go to a doctor there it will cost too much wait until you get home—I didn't know if the school had purchased travelling healthcare coverage. You then sent: "You're supposed to be my f---mother and you don't even care at all." That was my thanks.

When you got funding for university-three years of half my pension amount that I didn't have to sign permission for, my thank you was; "you're a fraudulent c---, I wish you were dead." Well if I ceased cessation the funds would cease right along with me.

My point...and I do have one, is how can I win when even my kindness offends you?!

When you girls were growing up I always told you your family is the people that function like family not those who are related to you by blood. "Blood's thicker than water," nepotists always say. I say blood may be thicker than water but so is bull crap. One day Rachel will realize that too and brand herself and her girlfriends with a matching tattoo and call it sisterhood by choice or some such.

It's looking like a lonely life out there for you. The men leave-oh, but you have such a good cover story. Well worn and over-used, but perfectly practiced: "they were abusive." Sorry honey-I know Alberta has a high rate of domestic abuse but I have been the recipient of your cruelty so many times now I find that along with your multitude of other lies hard to believe. If they are only abusive as a penalty for leaving...I have seen that used too.

"To forgive means to remember without the pain," someone said. If that is true, I am sitting here in total forgiveness in my newly decorated upper room office feeling quite blank of most emotions. But I think if you and I are ever to reconcile the past has to be buried without a map left or at the very least; only discussed in a therapeutic way.

What is helping me distance myself from the people that bug me is to say to myself; "they are not mine to fix."

And of course —never be mad at someone for being exactly who they are.

Forgive me Lord, if I am not asking "in faith, nothing wavering." Nothing seems to happen while I am believing! I am asking for you to do something about this in your own time and way—sure. And I believe. But I also am prepared and being given strength to go on with my life just fine the way it is. Because that is how good you are God. That is just how good you are. Amen."

Love just the same;

Mom

_____

_____

_____

"If you want God's help, keep it holy."—Grandma K

April 11, 2020

Dear Riley;

There is something wrong with all of us and if you think you are perfect, there's your something wrong talking. We are equal before God as far as His love and value of us goes.

Do you remember when you were growing up we had a sock basket and a snack cupboard? The basket sat close to the door because the first thing you girls ever did was pull your socks off and run around barefoot, then when we were going somewhere no one was ready. So I stationed a sock basket at the door and hardly ever did a pair match.

In my childhood we had a button box and every one told a story, each one represented the piece of clothing it had been cut off from and the purpose the item had been worn for. Nothing was ever thrown out until its last use was stripped from it.

I remember a ladies support group I used to attend nicknamed you "the anti-Christ." The weird thing was they were not religious people at all. In my distress moments, I ruefully, cynically, and bitterly refer to you as "my personal terrorist." But that is not faith nor forgiveness talking. I am admitting I am human and this is a roller coaster ride from hell.

You know, God prepared me to lose you long before it ever happened when I lost your older brother. He really has "been there before-understands how it feels." Paraphrased line from the Jeff and Sherri Easter song; "He's Been There." So it's okay if you don't come back to me, as long as you come back to God. That is peace talking. Perfect joy, and total peace, darling.

My prayer Father God, is first and foremost, that you bring Riley back to yourself. Cause her to have the Damascus Road Epiphany. Turn Saul into Paul again, or Paulette in this case. In Jesus Name, Amen.

In the gift stash/time capsule growing for you, I added a pendant that reminds me of something from The Hunger Games. I hated the series but you and Rachel liked it.

The Twilight Saga was another drag for me and thrill for you. Arrrrgh, lol.

Love, Mom

_____

_____

_____

"People don't read to see how Christians never have any problems and never make any mistakes; they need to see how God is bigger than our problems and more powerful than our mistakes."—Donna Parlow, Author of This Isn't the Life I Signed Up For.

April 12th, 2020

Dear Riley;

When I was pregnant with you I resented holding other children because all I wanted to do is hold you. And when I was expecting Rachel I could not imagine loving another child as much as you. I had to learn when you have children, you don't divide love, you multiply it.

Happy Easter. When we lived on B——— Road right on the edge of the lake, I was so broke for Easter I had to fit chocolate into the grocery budget but had nothing extra. I took our garbage to the dump myself and regularly gleaned from the share shed. I had furnished most of our home with whatever I could strap to the roof of my car, lol. Around that time, someone had donated two collectible dolls so I rigged a treasure hunt that ended in the yellow metallic bathroom of the trailer we lived in.

At the trailer in the G——— Mobile Home Park, I heard you crying and chanting in the bathtub to check and I heard: "Rachel! You farted right in my eye! You farted right in my eye!" And she had, bent over in the tub and let a one rip right in your face when picking up a toy. I laughed my ass off, no pun intended. Man she was a gassy kid sometimes, she was walking down the hallway one day and farted all the way—got exasperated and lamented: "Oh rippety-rip-rip!"

Love, Mom

"When you hurt people, they change right in front of you."—Me.

April 13th, 2020

Dear Riley;

There's book smarts and there's street smarts, to name two, and in my "books," survival smarts outrank formal education any day. I survived the streets of C thinking on my feet not nose in a book.

Gray hair is accumulating...the silverware used to be in a drawer...I had promised my new hairdresser I would stop frying my hair with drugstore box dye and now that the world is on isolation mode the "silverware" has moved upstairs. Rachel and my hairdresser reminded me I have ash blonde roots coming and it is technically grey but natural not aged.

Your step brother from a relationship said; "men age like wine, women age like milk." I could have killed him but for the truth. Men seem to carry age and weight better than we do.

My prayer is that the corona virus quarantine will still bring blessings for some, like if they needed a break and finally got one. There's an upside to most things.

The stain up there is from iced tea, by the way. You love it, it is what you and Rachel always order to drink in a restaurant.

Rachel and her boyfriend were just here, we talked about how to get your two boxes of childhood stuff to you. I have it packed and ready to go.

It sounds like her dad is now on his way out. Both of your fathers lived harsh, you know? So when you work hard, forget how to play, work some more, don't sleep enough, eat right or drink enough water...there you go. Literally.

Love, Mom

_____

_____

_____

"Tomorrow hopes we have learned something from yesterday."—John Wayne

April 14, 2020

Dear Riley;

You were always as smart as a whip, as the saying goes. That was evident as soon as you learned how to speak and that was early.

When I think about how poorly we lived though, I cringe. For the longest time there were no sheets on the beds, they had been torn up for toilet paper. You two could not fathom sleeping any other way. It's hard to change what you have always known.

What is weird is when I considered giving Rachel up for adoption at birth, the couple I had in mind split up and she would have been a child from a single parent home all the same. Does that mean we are simply destined for a certain life that cannot be changed?! I hope not.

I don't look at it as "woe is me," so much anymore, but rather as "wow is God." He brought us through incredible poverty and lack.

Your status card took your dad and I two years to wrangle out of Indian Affairs, and now I regret it. It will pay for a lifetime of education for some and the rest of us won't ever have had that opportunity, but we will probably get looked down on for a lack of education. Remind you of anything? I fought for that little white hunk of plastic so you could call me an: "uneducated @#$%." Well give me a status card sometime.

The government has got to stop throwing money at the aboriginal population in hopes of healing them. Since when does money heal?! Money seems to turn people into the biggest jerks. I have not met many wealthy that are also pleasant. Maybe that's why the Bible says "it is easier for a camel to go through the eye of a needle than for someone who is rich to enter the kingdom of God," Mark 10:25 (NIV) cuz He can't stand those clowns either!

I have been binge watching Longmire. There is a lot of Native American content in the series. It reminds me of you, although you are probably only 45 or less percent aboriginal.

Joke: how do the Polish bury their dead?

-With their buttocks sticking out of the ground so they have somewhere to park their pedal bikes.

Yes-I have found a culture cheaper than the dutch and the deutch. Who knew. And goodness knows if ya ain't deutch ya ain't moych." Just thought I would throw that in for free. We even have an extra vowel, woot woot. I used to say; "I'm a pure-bred German-I've got my papers!" As if I am a Pittbull fresh out of the dog breeders kennel (some days). But the truth is; "Let the one that boasts boast in the Lord." Jeremiah 9:24(NIV) Jesus is our only bragging right.

Love, Mom

_____

_____

_____

"Faith makes no provision for failure."–Unknown

"God only changes what you give Him."–Unknown

April 14, 2020

Dear Riley:

When I started this journal I thought I would do it for six months and then see how it felt. June 24th is the 6 month day. Perhaps I will close the cover of the book like the lid of a coffin and be done. There is tremendous peace in just being at one with whatever God has for you. Thanks to my Higher Power, it is well with my soul and my conscience.

I do not write with any concern about being right or wrong, politically or religiously correct. I write just to be.

These days I am publishing books. It is pretty exciting stuff and it is good to be able to share it with someone, even like this. And the one up on Amazon is available globally. I hope my novels are the next thing to go viral, lol.

The journal will be published also, with names changed of course.

There is even peace about my ever finding a soulmate, after almost 30 years of either searching or involved with the wrong man.

Outside, the yard is dripping with rain and full of work, just waiting for me. I can't wait. There is something so rewarding in spring cleanup.

One day I will just buy this place and restore the old hotel. Or convert it into a bed and breakfast. Or both. Gotta run.

Love, Mom

_____

_____

_____

"To build may have to be the slow and laborious task of years. To destroy can be the thoughtless act of a single day."—Winston Churchill

"God can use all things for good, even sin."—Winston Churchill

April 15th, 2020

Dear Riley;

With Easter being here I found I still wanted to buy gifts in twos, because that it how it always was. I had two little girls to look after. Rachel always insists on an egg for Easter; and she mock threatens me with a penalty if I don't get her one. Personally I do not see the connection between the crucifixion of Christ and chocolate and I am one who can find an excuse for it anytime usually. At one time I even stored chocolate in the first aide kit. Well? I have THOSE kind of emergencies, lol. Shoot me.

It is hard to watch you pretend to connect with your sister and then to pull the plug; "if you don't get rid of mom." That is out and out emotional abuse and blackmail. And here you are such a crusader for social work and protecting children from abuse. One day and make it soon Lord—let the real truth come out and set more than few people free of lies. Amen. That was a double conversation but it isn't like the Lord doesn't hear it all anyway: "God will bring every deed into judgment, including every hidden thing, whether it is good or whether it is evil." Ecclesiastes 12:13-14. (NIV).

"Every deed is a seed and comes back treed," I always say. There you go. Now it's Biblical.

I remember once when we were living in the Bronx of R---- for the second time, I texted you to say; "hey little girl, how's it going?" And you said; "I'm not your little girl, so don't call me that." Then when I tried to tell you that comment hurt deeply, you sent back a spam of; "hahahahahahahahahahahahahahahahahahahaha."

"Your daughter traumatizes you," a psychiatrist told me yesterday. You have done things I never taught you and somehow, I am always the bad guy and all your problems are my fault somehow. I can't help but think about you being a kid from a convict who was meaner than a four eyed snake. I finally cut off the phone I was paying for you to text harass me with and then your dad got all up in it. I snapped at him; "Bruce-ya finally wanna get involved? Tell your demon spawn to smarten up." I had had it! But that wasn't the thing to say either. I was exhausted so much of the time.

In some of your cards and artwork to me you signed them; "love, your papoose from Bruce." Its hard to imagine you ever loved me, but I try and realize you are sick.

And in my most bitter moment, I think; "just think—a little bit of racism would have saved me a whole pile of grief..!" I would have stayed away from dating an aboriginal. But I don't want to be a bigot or a redneck, never was. Then in my lowest point of pain; "Mary had a kid from God and I guess I had one from the devil."

A ladies group I used to go to called you the Antichrist. And none of them were religious.

My counsellor says it sounds like you were the kid who was always pushing the envelope. A problem child from day one. A walking conduct disorder.

It is going to be hard to get anything done legally across the spawn of two police services but if I have to get a restraining or no contact order I will. Tough love is tough and I should have utilized it sooner instead of writing excuses for you to take to school for teachers trying to deal with you. Now to turn this thing around...I have to remember the Isaiah Word: "not by might, nor by power, but by my spirit says the Lord."

It's hard to reread this and hear forgiveness. It easy to hear the punitive, toxic legalists I booted out of my life clucking their tongues in disapproval. "It should only be love and kindness..." Oh I have tried kindness. It enables in this case because there is addiction involved.

It's time for tough love. And things are going to get real tough before they get better methinks. I am making "prayments" on this situation. It doesn't mean no one ever had to pick up a stick and smack a rock, like Moses. I used to do nothing but fight for you two girls and myself for survival. Now I am fighting for the safety of my mental health.

Lord-guide me and show me what to do. Thank you and Amen.

Love, Mom

_____

_____

_____

"You will learn the best lessons in life when you are defeated."-Unknown

April 16th, 2020

Dear Riley;

It is hard to talk about you when my memories of your childhood are fading and there is no relationship. I remember your incredibly small, sweet birdlike voice saying: "op-it?" for "open it?" And "moy, moy," for "more, more?" when you were a toddler.

Your voice stayed pretty well a butterfly whisper and you would get mad at me for asking you to repeat yourself.

In the book I am writing based on my frigged up life-I mean, interesting life, I am up to my pregnancy with you. It was as if you would never get here and the gestation cycle would last indefinitely, lol. I could not wait to meet you.

But if I ever raised children again they would have to be boys. No offence.

Around here they are all about breeding, long after anyone's prime years. I dubbed it the "make-your-own-grandchild-program." It is a good thing though, that the young men want to raise a family instead of the make'em and shake'em schedule so many men have going.

Your dad struggled with alcohol and drug addictions, as you know, but he lived long enough to kick the sauce and that was huge. My theory is the guy with the P.H.D worked no less harder than the one that finally overcame an addiction. I sometimes say "I have a P.H.D.; a Personal Hell Diploma." But that sounds like a victim.

Love, Mom

_____

_____

_____

"We are what we repeatedly do. Excellence then is not an act, but a habit." –Aristotle

"Integrity is doing the right thing even when no one is watching." –C.S.Lewis

April 17th, 2020

Dear Riley;

You were such a tiny baby, barely over six pounds and oh, what a head of hair!

I just found this scripture: "The Lord your God walks throughout your camp to protect you and deliver your enemies to you; so your encampments must be holy." Deuteronomy 23:14 (HSCB).

Also: "These are the borders of the land you are getting as an inheritance." Numbers 34:2 (MSG).

See? There is a lot of native spirituality in the Bible. I was always a sucker for their colouring, in fact, you're here because someone had brown eyes...dark chocolate.

I pray God heals your rejection wound. All of them, but the rejection wound for sure. Amen.

Remember the serenity prayer...to change what you can but don't worry about what you can't. Pick your battles because there is no way they are all yours–in fact they are God's. Learn from other's mistakes...you won't live long enough to make them all yourself.

There is a possibility Rachel can deliver the two boxes of stuff I have of yours, baby books and such. I don't want to see any of it again unless its on good terms. It beats sending it all the way eight to twelve hours north to your K grandparents and then having them mail it just past my address to you when we live two hours apart.

Love, Mom

_____

_____

_____

"Don't tell God how big your storm is, tell your storm how big your God is." –Unknown

April 18th, 2020

Dear Riley;

Will society ever return to normalcy? As if normal was ever more than a setting on the blender. Will there be a season of reconnection? I doubt it. We may become a people of P.P.E. and avoiding eye contact as if social snottery was ever a deterrent to a virus.

Isn't it strange–I think us three–you, Rachel, myself, are workaholics, and when one works 5 jobs you think; "if only I had some time..." Then when the time comes and hangs heavy on your hands you stare at the clock and curse under your breath...and wonder how you will manage to stay sane...sanity is for losers though.

There are some who say that covid 19 is "a sign of the times, the end is near," but the end has been near all my life. And I am 44 now. Well good if it is the end of the world–beam me up as they say on Star Trek.

If it was Biblical, I'd say when your Grandmother F dies she is going straight to heaven cuz she's already been through hell. But it doesn't work that way. That is like the phrases; "God won't give you more than you can handle," and: "God helps those who help themselves."

This house was teeming with spiritual activity when I first moved in and gradually, over the course of the year, I have cleansed it of spirits. There is power in the name of Jesus. Now it needs to be delivered of too much stuff!

Love, Mom

_____

_____

_____

"It took me a long time to learn that you are allowed to do what is best for you even if it upsets other people." – Aunty Acid

April 19, 2020

Dear Riley;

Did you know the birth process alone is a loss? So in that sense we are born experienced. Loss is inevitable.

I am relieved to say anyone I ever thought I had to have in life I didn't actually need at all.

Wasn't that sad after the La Loche shooting when the father of one of the boys had to dig his own son's grave. Maybe he wanted to, like for a sense of purpose or one last thing he could do for his child. But oh, how that grieved me.

Losing a child to rebellion has got to be the worst form of loss. It feels like I am always at a funeral and the gilded lid never gets closed.

Last night the basement flooded, I could tell by the smell of moist dirt and the line on the wall where the water had been up to. It's like living in the old testament.

There is already green in my flower bed. Spring is here! This is the awkward stage where you want to clean the yard so bad but you'll end up raking the last of the snow if you don't wait for the final melt off, and I am foursquare against raking snow.

I wonder if at some point your heart gets so dead toward someone you once loved that it just never feels again for that person. Like emotional leprosy. Sometimes that is my wish; total numbness.

Mom

_____

_____

_____

"Butterflies can't see their wings. They can't see how truly beautiful they are, but everyone else can. People are like that as well." Naya Rivera

April 20th, 2020

Dear Riley;

Today the knife twisted in my gut and challenged my resolve not to suffer but to experience. Your Aunt M2 always says; "the body will accept what the mind rejects." It is a grief day, even though not necessarily thinking about you. My body let me know I was grieving by pain and difficulty moving. And these times are necessary as part of the journey and growing through circumstances rather than letting them define you and leave you stuck.

My friend said; "focus on music, it's healing." Amen to that! Music is a universal language. I am trio-lingual as long as only being able to sing the third language counts.

When we get to the next life, if your grandmother doesn't get sainthood in heaven I am going to throw a fit. A temper tantrum at the pearly gates perhaps, because she has had such a rough life all her life. The man she is married to, your father fought him off of her several times, many times, trying to protect his mom. He told me how he had vowed not to become like that and ended up that way himself. That's how it works; or doesn't. You don't overcome by focusing hard on turning from something, you zero in on something different, period.

Seems all my life I have fought for my place in this world and you too, but we have a place or we wouldn't be here.

You start healing the moment you are injured, someone told me about a physical injury. I hope it is true for any wound, emotional, spiritual, or physical. Dr. Phil says time alone doesn't even heal it depends on what happens during that time.

This town—the one I walk everyday times three, felt hostile again this morning. There is a lot of sinless perfection walking around here with its nose in the air. Better them than I, I'd hate to put that kind of pressure to perform on myself. There's a good scripture about that; 2 Corinthians 10: 12 (NIV) "Of course we would not dare classify ourselves or compare ourselves with those who rate themselves so highly. How stupid they are! They make up their own standards to measure themselves by, and they judge themselves by their own standards!" Well that is one way to win the contest. But what a bunch of stiffs the one bunch is.

Christians believe in abstaining from sex before marriage, and I know a couple that has been dating and dating for years without any sign of a ring or rumour of commitment...she "serves" in church and is deeply "enfriended," (word I invented) with a corrupt church leader. She also runs the overhead gizmo while glaring down at whoever she dislikes on appearances and judges someone who cusses but is quite content not to get her legal screwing rights. See? I can be judgmental too...therefore I should fit right in. Besides I only cuss in German! But it isn't good to judge the judgmental. Because judgmental is still mental. You follow?

Someone sat right next to me at a Bible study (gossip night) and oooohed and ahhhed about how we should pray about the alcoholism in this town— well the trouble is the alkies need something to take the edge off their painful experiences with the pharisees and the self righteous grunts.

"For it is when the Lord thinks well of a person that he is really approved, and not when he thinks well of himself." 2 Corinthians 10:18 (NIV). Amen hallelujah, dats preachin to da choir!

And on the bright side of the north gate behind the red barn, I just distracted myself from my own pain which is perhaps why they all judge to start with. See? We are all as bad as the people we complain about.

I remember the first time I told you about the whore in Revelations, you kind of obsessed over it; "the church is a whore, the church is a whore."

Love, Mom

_____

_____

_____

"Don't let nobody who ain't been in your shoes, tell you how to tie your laces."–Unknown

"Wear my shoes for a mile–they will pinch your feet."–Me

April 27th, 2020

Dear Riley;

One should not leave church until one has made change in the offering plate and spiked the communion juice with Tabasco sauce, really put that ––––on everything. Just saying. But like a country song I am the leaving kind...especially an organization where single woman are so judged and men worshipped. "church," has become my new cuss-word and I make no apology for my opinions or potty mouth. Deal with it or don't.

I've gone dead on some deep levels, I'm not feeling sorry for myself, just stating the facts...of course with C.P.T.S.D., there will be disconnection at times. It's a welcome lack of feeling, a kind of emotional leprosy. A numbness where throbbing pain once thrived.

Well I hope you holed up with your grandma F during this quarantine, and caught up with her.

Once the two apple crate boxes go to you there won't be much of you around here anymore.

I don't know how someone can live with lacerating their own mother's soul the way you have. But not much hurts anymore. Scar tissue is like that.

Soon life will be busier and that always helps.

The snow is almost all gone, so all the debris from last winter is uncovered. Winter covers a multitude of sin and spring reveals them, ha ha. I poked around out there some today in the dirt and in the sun. Great fun.

Goodnight;

Mom

_____

_____

_____

"Then the one who sits on the throne said "And now I make all things new!" He also said to me, "Write this, because these words are true and can be trusted." Rev. 21:5 (GNB)

April 22, 2020

Dear Riley;

Your great grandmother P wrote everything in red pen, that was her deal. She wasn't a schoolmarm or anything...mother of ten children, but she wrote in red when she wasn't gardening or giving birth.

There are some tough broads in your family tree to be sure. Helen, the red ink scribe and mother of ten was married to a ballistic drunk who was only home ten times in their lifetime if you know what I mean. None of us know for sure what all happened in their marriage besides ten kids and flagrant misery, but life with a drunk while pregnant and scrubbing socks on a washboard can't have been easy. Grandpa P died young and alone of liver failure and even managed to squeak out a deathbed confession asking for God's forgiveness. That and calling the name of the woman he had abused all their life together. So we will see him in heaven. But there is no guarantee for any of us that we will have that kind of deathbed chance. I heard a joke once about how a man learned every good deed we commit is converted to the construction of our "heavenly home, hence we will not live in cookie cutter abodes up there. When he gets there he sees his late wife in a nice house but he is led to a simple cabin. When he asks the Lord why He replies; "you didn't send up enough building materials."

Great Grandma K, was no slouch at hard work and babies either, she had thirteen while gardening. Ha ha. She also developed skin cancer a few times before it spread and took her at an old age. Grossmama (German for Grandma) K always wore a wide brimmed straw hat over her kerchief to work outside and still developed carcinoma. She fared a lot better in husband than did Grandma Helen P. She was married to my favourite soul, Grandpa K and I still miss him. That man could hug you with words and make you feel accepted where Grossmam had her detached style with most people most times and it frustrated some of her daughter-in-laws.

You come from tough women, strong farmers, and prayer warriors. Woo hoo! And hiya-ho!

Love, Mom

_____

_____

_____

"Stop your crying and wipe away your tears, all that you have done for your children will not go unrewarded: they will return from the enemies land. There is hope for your future, your children will come back home. I, the Lord, have spoken. Jeremiah 31: 16, 17 (GNB)

April 23rd, 2020

Dear Riley;

If I missed you once I have missed you a thousand times.

Today was another heavy day, the sky was grey and I was blue. An Alan Jackson country song.

I took a temporary one month job for some more to do to fill up the emptiness and I don't mean just my bank account. Some of this shut down is creating work. What a life this is turning out to be. As I made my lunch for tomorrow I was grateful that at least there wasn't a grown man sending me to work while he stayed home and played wifey. It triggers me that financial abuse is considered only when "he doesn't let you get a job." HAH. How about when he refuses to get one and runs to mop the floor when I ask him to get a job as if that is what I meant. That kind of domestic abuse feels the same as being smacked around, like being cheated on is the same as being cheated out of what you need in a relationship. I remember you said it so well once about abusive romance; "there is a vending machine that doles out cookies, but it switches to crap every once in a while until you find yourself collecting turds waiting for the rare pastry. And the desserts get fewer and further between. Only you worded it much better. I suppose you blame me for your experiences in relationships too. I got the powah—I sat up in the sky above Alberta and waved my wand while chanting: "let every man be a domestic abuser—even in casual friendship." As if.

What I am responsible for is ignoring the vibes or the lack of any and proceeding anyway. That is on me—and those things just became reasons to leave within a short time anyway. I always had the great boundary talk with men about how I was sexually abused and how I would be danged and hanged before I keep anyone's dirty secret. And I trained you both to talk about everything. Then when Rachel was 14 she was still abused. The hardest thing was going along with what she wanted done— which was nothing. She had already quit being alone with him, but I couldn't keep his picture after that. T handled it great— financial abuser and drunk that he was—he said do whatever you have to do.

It has been 30 years of crappy experiences with men now. Rachel seems to think she finally has a keeper now and he is nice— I have met him. Hopefully you find a safe man to be with—and hopefully you become a safe person yourself. Anyone who abuses her own mother...that is a hard scene to take no matter what your excuse is.

It would be hard to get the law involved if there is any more hate contact and harassment, but I am willing to do what it takes. At some point my life counts for something also.

Oh God change this already. Amen.

Love, Mom

_____

_____

_____

"Everybody is famous in a small town."–Miranda Lambert country song.

"They have to talk about you because when they talk about themselves no one listens."–Unknown

April 24, 2020

Dear Riley:

Well I am a little perturbed-off to say the least. I found out you have been following me on Instagram so I blocked you. You cannot have it both ways, verbally abuse your own mother, tell her you wish she was dead and that you would throw her body in a ditch upon her demise...would refuse to buy a coffin even....tell me your grandmother F is your mother...which makes your father your brother. And if you don't think that is a problem...

We will never have a relationship until you show a sign, an inkling, a some kind of resemblance of being able to show me any kind of respect. And I suspect the bar is too low right there. There needs to be a ton of more changes before anything changes.

I am not beneath you despite your grand delusions of greatness regardless of behaviour. I will not be auditioning for a part in your charmed life at all. I have given you all I could give all your life when I could and only to get sh–– on as the check clears the bank. Even now you receive funding from my via my pension because you are in school and I could have refused to sign the paperwork. You have caught on to the stereotypical attitude of a certain race that you are owed no matter what the behaviours and it needs to stop.

The problem has never been my generosity. No sirree.

Soon I will give back what I can find of your pictures, report cards, baby memorabilia, artwork. There's an extra copy of the family picture we last did but I doubt you would want it. Unity is the last thing you strive for.

There are reasons I pray for you. Many many reasons. You need deliverance of bondage to anger, and that demonic spirituality you so believe in.

You said I would never see my grandchildren. I prayed there would not even be any at this rate.

As far as the disposal of my body goes after I pass; the joke is on you. I am going to be turned into a pick your part and then sent to a body farm to see how well I decompose under a tree. Maybe even in a ditch.

I wish you could just be a miserable little b-with-an-itch in your therapists office and leave me alone. Just a thought.

Tough love, Mom

_____

_____

_____

"God weeps along with man, and takes him by the hand, tears are a language God understands."—Song by Aimee Lambert

April 25th, 2020

Dear Riley;

Today I woke up wondering how God can be so cruel as to expect a mother to wait for her child to be saved. Then I realized that first of all, you are His more than mine on loan to me, that He "ever liveth to make intercession for them," (Heb 7:25, KJV) and "God weeps along with man." Jesus wept. John 11:35 (NIV). Then I thanked Big Daddy for restoring my relationship with Rachel when she was swept away into her father's fables. Ohhh I have watched my children get abducted spiritually and emotionally and it is not fun. I told the Lord there had better never be two sets of footprints in the sand or just mine, because I will need him to carry me until the end of time.

I am not mad about the social media thing anymore. Just a bit ago I heard you laughing in my memory. A soft tinkling laugh like your great Gramma K.

Sin is ultimately against God. What we do wrong against people we ultimately do against Him and the things people do against us are offensive to him. The Bible says: "The insults that are hurled against you have fallen on me." Romans 15:3 (NIV). It is hard to remember that in a heated moment though. Just yesterday I told someone to go somewhere privately and do something private at her earliest convenience. (And I repented while noting that for me that is still huge progress) After she took my head off for not wearing the obviously reused face shield she offered me and after she had not even taken my temperature. The corona virus provides an opportunity for rudeness in the guise of saving lives. Yay.

Remember how I used to go and go all day? Well not anymore. Not since the nervous breakdown. Maybe it is a gift. Someone told me once that I would die young if I kept it up. Well that which doesn't kill you turns out to be a good thing. Actually I often say: "that which doesn't kill you only makes you more alive in Christ."

The truth will set you free of almost anything if you are rigorously honest with yourself, God, and another human being. Even if the truth is inconvenient, and it it most times. I have discovered though that the truth also sets you free of the people that cannot handle the truth. Oh well. I was social distancing long before it was a thing. I am prepared to keep it up.

See, when God created us for relationship it was chiefly for one with Himself; all others are secondary. Gary Smalley puts it well in his book: The D.N.A. Of Relationships; 'the kingdom of heaven is all about relationships," but; "God is the author of life, people and things are just a bonus." It starts and ends with Him.

You always were an obstinate little turkey. Even as a baby your first expression was glaring at the nurses when they woke you up from a jaundiced sleep. Don't beg. Differ. Lol. That is your mantra. And differ for the sake of differing if nothing else.

Love, Mom

_____

_____

_____

"Better a live dog than a dead lion." -Doug Bachelor

Courage doesn't always roar, sometimes it's the quiet voice at the day whispering "I will try again tomorrow."-

Mary Anne Radmacher

April 27th, 2020

Dear Riley;

Today I asked God to give me His love where ever I felt pain and before long I was giggling. How cool is God?!

I can just hear people thinking; bipolar disorder. But when you are purebred German you are way past that.

We are intense people-we started the 2nd world war. Not that I was there...but now the peeps I struggle with the most are guess who and what. Yup. Deutchlinders. (Germans. High Germans, to be exact). The brutal bunch. We need to be mixed in with other breeds- watered down really. Well it turns out I am. The ancestry spit-kit came back making me only 70 percent Deutch and the rest Swedish-Russian.

Mother's Day is coming. It's hard for us Moms who have estranged children. Or deceased children. Even if our best parenting efforts sucked. We are all broken somehow, is my theory, and if you think you are sinless perfection there is your brokenness talking. Loudly. It constitutes a delusion of grandiosity which is a symptom of bipolar disorder.

Do you remember the "living room church" we attended briefly. That was another rich man with the corresponding personality. Ahem! Anyway, I swear he had "high-polar disorder," always so happy and yippy you wanted to either slap him or help him scrub that "Cyril Sneer," grin off his face with a wire brush. Like who is genuinely always giddy?!

Last year Rachel and I spent some time in this house when I was moving into it. Hard to believe it's been a year in this once haunted hotel. I have cleansed it.

There will be repetition in this book, did I mention that there will be repetition? Ha ha. It is the language of trauma, but once again, I chose not to suffer. It is simply part of the journey.

I am glad you got out of R----. What a town, although such a pretty city in so many ways. Now if Rachel could find it within herself to get outta there so I can quit worrying about her safety and that of my future grandchildren. It isn't a place to raise children.

Miss you.

Love, Mom

"The things that break your heart can fix your vision."–

–Unknown

April 28th, 2020

Dear Riley;

Do you think you will go through life collecting careers like I did?

Today, I wrote your birthday on the calendar as if I needed a reminder of the day my body was ripped open to expel you. I have permanent scars I can still feel in the bathtub if I move wrong. And I won't see you...but there it is, marked on the wall and on my body.

Woo-hoo this yard is really taking shape. Those ugly blue-grey garden boxes that look like coffins from a Western movie really have to go as does the ugly doghouse and the unsightly bench. When I get through chainsawing through this museum of ugly yard artifacts someone will be able to have their wedding here. Or will want to...

It will be hard to pass up all of your pictures and everything of you. Then sometimes I wish I had never had you–and I don't feel guilty about it because even God regretted having children...Genesis 6: 6 (GNB) "He was so filled with regret that He had ever made them and put them on the earth." That was right before the flood.

It is hard—but what isn't, to come to C and know we are in the same city and there is not going to be any contact. We are simply two out of a million people there.

The worst parents I know of have children that will deny the domestic abuse and take a bullet for the parent who threatened and/or beat them every day of their lives even though that parent would not do the same for them. So don't anybody give me the delusion that every good parent has a good relationship with their children and every bad parent doesn't. Look at all the _____ your father pulled and you idolize him.

God sent me two friends that have lost children, specifically daughters, to rebellion. No one has to be alone unless they want to be.

Well I have to go study for my private investigations course.

Love, Mom

_____

_____

_____

"Every storm over your head is still under God's feet."–Unknown

"The Lord makes firm the steps of the one who delights in him." Psalm 37:23 (NIV)

April 29th, 2020

Dear Riley;

Your stepfather is definitely on his way out. He has gone to our mutual hometown to die. Both you and Rachel's father will have died young. Someone called it karma, but I call it reaping and sowing. It sounds a lot like Korsakoff's Syndrome, but then he would be able to overcome it with huge doses of vitamin B if I remember my medical training.

I wish I had experienced the loyalty you both showed Daddy. No bitterness there. Oh no. I worked too hard top raise you and provide for you to be betrayed like that, ABUSED like that. If I had to raise children again I would wonder a) if God loved me, and b) insist on boys.

Mostly though, I think about how I would throw myself in front of a speeding semi to save your lives, you and Rachel's. A human wheel chock. I don't worry about you or anyone else throwing me under the bus anymore, I simply park there.

Everything you accuse people of you have something of yourself, you spot it you've got it. Takes it to know it, whatever you say that's what you are. You call me a narcissist, I see every symptom of a Malignant Narcissist in you. No conscience, no concept of violating others, me me me, I-me-my-mentality. Cruel and vicious. A user of people. If there was a personality disorder beyond grace–this is the one I would nominate. But no one is past saving or being salvageable by God.

Love, Mom

_____

_____

_____

"Be careful not to measure your holiness by other people's sins."–Martin Luther

"Judgmental is still mental."–Me

April 30th, 2020

Dear Riley;

It's hard to make the connection between protecting you from "monsters," when you were little and then watching you become one. You have done things you never witnessed me do.

I don't imagine if you ever read this book that you'll like it much. Remember the truth will set you free but first it will tick you off.

These days I have more patience...must be an age thing. The front licence plate on my first car said: "Patience my ass, I'm gonna kill someone." The slogan nowadays should read: "Taking offence when there is none being given is theft." And people who are always taking offence should really get that checked.

I grew up with a poster of a missing girl whose parents never found out what had happened to her. Her father died not knowing, the mom stayed behind on the farm where they had raised her with nothing left but photos of her child. I will never forget Caroline. At least you're alive and I know where you live, kind of. Not knowing must be its own torture.

The world is beautiful and green again, how my arms ache like a country song from loving up this yard, lol.

When the world opens up again I will send your stuff up with Rachel. Hopefully it will be a treasure hunt for you in the apple boxes.

Please save my daughter Lord. And me from bitterness and unforgiveness. Amen.

Love, Mom

"On my darkest days, when I feel inadequate, unloved and unworthy, I remember whose daughter I am and straighten my crown." —Unknown

May 1st, 2020

Dear Riley;

I am starting to measure time in failed relationships; "that was three jerks ago..." Lol. Not good.

Yesterday T told me; "I lost me when I lost you." So write the next country hit...that is sick. Aren't we all individuals regardless? When I was married briefly to D I watched my identity fade away. I became someone's wife and someone's stepmother, even after the split I was someone who used to be married to...who used to drive the station wagon......and none of that misrepresentation was me.

I hope you find a high powered love. I also hope you discover a higher power's love.

Most days are filled with peace about you. It is the neatest thing to place you in God's hands and leave you there.

Your artwork was precocious, how I miss the unique use of colour.

I miss you, but I even have peace if you never come back. Love, Mom

_____

_____

_____

"God is good all the time and all the time God is good."–Unknown

"God is good in spite of me."–Unknown

May 2nd, 2020

Dear Riley;

By the time your father passed we had no relationship left and my initial reaction was coldness, I admit. You have to realize though, anytime you didn't have the source in front of you, anything you hear or see from a distance will be compromised at least. So it really wasn't fair to you to respond to my alleged reaction with such vicious cruelty after your sister blabbed it. Don't believe everything you hear and half of what you see.

You need to understand your relationship with your father was unique to you two, and he was never my father so there were different dynamics. By the time he died we were hated each other. Although God and I are working hard on eliminating hatred from my life.

Now the other father is on his way out and I am trying to prepare your sister. You can't abuse yourself with alcohol and drugs and poor nutritional and health habits and expect to live a long and healthy life. He thinks he will beat cancer a second time and granted, he and your father–the personality twins from across a vast spectrum of cultures—were tough buggers. But no—this is IT. Everyone around him knows that.

Cold wind slicing through to my soul is keeping me in the house along with the pandemic. Planned demic as far as I say. It seems staged—but on the bright side "the Chinese finally made something that lasted," the gas pump attendant told me. His daughter was horrified while I giggled. You can't say those kind of things out loud any more.

I am quite the conspiracy theorist, and no one need expect an apology for it cuz there is none coming.

Love, Mom

_____

_____

_____

"It is easier to ask for forgiveness than permission."—Unknown

"Attitudes count more than achievements."—Rick Warren

May 3rd, 2020

Dear Riley;

The pup is taking the liberty of digging in my flower bed. He is lucky he is cute! So we compromised...he can have the grass side of the porch and leave me the flower side.

Relationships continue to suck if there is one, although I am sure giving it carbon dioxide doesn't help. I can't get the maybe out of my mouth; can't develop a crush without getting burned. Yet scriptures say; "I know the you can do all things; no purpose of yours can be thwarted." Job 42:2 (BSB)

It's Mother's Day in a week, a difficult holiday for many, so I try and bless them. When life hurts God is in the pain and He never wastes it.

We have what God wants us to have and we can't lose what He gives us unless he takes it away. Make sense?

I pray for you often.

Love, Mom

_____

_____

"If suffering perfects the soul, someone is trying to make a saint out of me!"–Unknown

May 3rd, 2020

Dear Riley;

When you were a baby I napped you three times a day and then you grew up to handle as many jobs sometimes. Maybe the structure did something for you. Maybe I did something right. Then again you are a raging insomniac like me...

Your Grandma K has her wisdom, and some of it is low German but it'll translate...

"If it falls apart that easily there is nothing falling apart yet."

"He who drives fast won't see it and he who drives slow thinks its all good."

"No is an answer to."

Here's another one from I–don't know where: "if we all knew exactly what the other person thought, none of us would be friends. How true is that.

Outside, the weather is under the weather. Thank God we didn't have to drive today. That box truck feels like a box kite in elements like this.

I am learning when you are down to just God, you are in the prime condition to realize God is enough and that only He will get you through anyway. Nothing and no one else will.

Currently your sister and I are annoying each other, lol. Her texts are evasive and my pushing is as the G.P.S. voice says: "Not sure how to help with that." Rachel told me casually the one day; "did you know when you were working night shift I took the truck and went for a drive?" Gaaaaaasp. No licence to drive...ooooh my. That old Ford Explorer was a loan to me even! The things that could have happened. "Oh and then there was the time we all skipped school and went to Saskatchewan." Wow. Single parenting of teenagers...don't try this at home folks.

I both thank God and pray for you girls' safety. Now I am glad I did and still do. Furrrig!

Love, Mom

_____

_____

_____

"If my life is fruitless, it doesn't matter who praises me, and if my life is fruitful it doesn't matter who criticizes me." John Bunyan

May 5th, 2020

Dear Riley;

All the years your step father mocked and made fun of me and then called me crazy, he is now unable to be alone because his mind is going. He fades in and out of reality. The problem is he is probably too far gone to realize he is reaping what he has sown.

In my book; "Growing Up Men," I am about to write about going into labour with you. For an entire day plus two hour and a quarter hours. If motherhood was oing to be easy it would have been started with labour. That was a major clue right there.

For my entire life I heard "the end is near." Lately, it seems it really is all wrapping up. Fires, floods, diseases, your worst enemies being from your own household, daughter against mother, check check check! My neighbour is cutting his grass and is unaware of my eight year old's bedtime...what's even better is that turbo-charged lawn tractor is lacking a muffler. Oh well, we four all get along famously. We are four single people living by ourselves in four houses on the same block. There is something in the water here I think.

I cannot forget when the text came through last January for us to pray for the woman's wife's hee hoo because it wasn't healing right after their 11th baby. Like let's not leave anything to the imagination here...oh my friend and I had a field day with that! We would slip it into conversations at the most unorthodox moment; "and could you please pray for so-and so's hoo hah?! —yes, name it and claim it—barf sound—no thank you." Lol. It was sooo bad and sooooo hilarious, made funnier by pantomiming around pretending to limp with a wounded middle part...oh we were so bad. We really must fight human nature harder than we do. Especially when it almost gets you kicked out of the local coffee shop.

There is a geographical cure and make no mistake about it. It is a cabin by the lake with boat access only.

Today I heard you laughing but I had to try harder than last time I think. Hopefully I will always be able to remember.

Love, Mom

_____/_____

_____

_____

"If money is the root of all evil I must be a saint!"—Unknown

May 6th, 2020

Dear Riley;

Whoever said, "if ya got nuttin nice to say don't say it at all," can get fried. Somethings have to be said because the truth, no matter how ugly, can only liberate. "Secrets are lies and bad manners besides," was another quote I grew up with.

Then later, in counselling/therapy/group support I learned; "openness is to wholeness as secrets are to sickness." Amen to that.

I hope, when you become a mother, that your children don't cause you more pain than joy. But if they do, give it to God and realize grandchildren are a parents' revenge.

When you girls were growing up I often told you; "your family is the people who function like family, not simply those related to you." Amen to myself.

I am learning reaping is no respector of persons or perpetrator. Like for example, if you take a baseball bat to a known offender, you will get beaten at some point. Only harder, because those who sow wind reap a storm.

Karma pays back with interest. We are ALWAYS responsible for ourselves, no matter what we have experienced. And the "other guys" human rights never dry up, even if sometimes it seems they should.

Love, Mom

_____

_____

_____

"Never let what you feel change what you know." –Me

May 7th, 2020

Dear Riley;

Today is your Aunt M2's 49th birthday. Not that you have a relationship with her, we are a small, disjointed family. I will refer to her as M2 since both my sisters/ your aunts names start with M. They were always close and I was the odd man out. Don't have three kids.

The saying "three is a crowd," is partially true. It didn't work well when I had you and Rachel and a step daughter.

Then when my younger and only brother came along I hoped the score would even out and I would have a buddy and we were close but he drifted over to M2 so I am still the odd man out in the family. Us four siblings hardly ever all get along at the same time and isn't that a tad sad? If I was the whole entire problem why does it bug me so much?

This July your K Grandparents are on their 50th wedding anniversary. We are going to give them credit for time served anyway.

I am losing steam on the dream of a love story, a lasting love, romance, and commitment. Holy crap that's four guys already! Reminds me of the joke I told you earlier.

A drunk stumbles through a graveyard and stops to try and read a headstone. "Doting father, loving husband, and loyal friend," one said. "Holy ————!" he exclaims. "They've got three guys in the same hole!" Lol. And I wonder why I am single? Hee hee.

Another joke: what do a thousand battered men have in common? (They didn't listen). Originally it is battered women but I thought I'd switch it up.

Since the nervous breakdown I have been losing hair like I just had a baby and there is no baby. Hair is a big deal when you are a woman, especially one who was raised Mennonite..."a woman's hair is her glory." These days I am glory-compromised.

Your Grandpa K sure likes to tell stories and jokes. I guess that is where I got it from. That and talking with my hands like an Italian.

Love, Mom

_____

_____

_____

"I'm a king's kid."—Me

May 8th, 2020

Dear Riley;

If I had known all these years of raising you would pay off to an "I just want Daddy" attitude...I went without things I needed so you girls could have the things you wanted, laid on the living room floor so you could each have a bedroom. Whoever said hard work and sacrifice paid off can go pound either salt or sand—I offer flexible options. Apparently being the absent and otherwise abusive, angry parent is what pays off. Good to know.

The Bible says "for your labour is not in vain in the Lord." These days I feel as if it was all for nothing with you, and feelings are nor criminal. It's what we do with them that matters.

Okay—okay—I am under control now and slightly less bitter.

I remember when you figured out how to make white bread and butter taste like chicken by putting seasoning salt on it. And how you and Rachel used to sing out "awkward!" over something, well, awkward. Or how you would say profound, poignant things and add "I feel smart."

Do you remember playing with My Little Pet Shop toys and fighting over the accessories with Rachel. You were both into that and Polly Pocket for a while, how those little tiny pieces would get all over the place and anywhere but together after a while. The vacuum had a steady diet, lol.

Did you know it is a Mennonite tradition to put a plank in the middle of the bed and have a dating couple stay on their prospective side of the bed and talk all night? It was to enforce the don't let the sun go down upon your wrath scripture; to get them practised in talking things through. And because you are a "Germindianeuchite" this story applies to you.

If I had realized that your childhoods would be a fart in the wind I might have done things differently. I wish I had spent more time with you. Now there isn't even time to make up in adulthood because of your addiction to this anger toward me. It seems to be insatiable, hence why I call it addiction.

I miss reading stories, cuddling and tickle fights. They say Grandchildren are a parents second chance, but not at this rate.

Love, Mom

_____

_____

_____

"The moment you master emotional intelligence, the game changes."–Unknown

"Thoughts become things."–Unknown

May 9th, 2020

Dear Riley;

I developed a gut ache writing about the twenty six hours of labour with you, so I think I captured it well. Brutal is the word. A definite fore-shadowing of things to come.

If we ever have a relationship again we will have to agree to avoid certain topics I guess, and I hate tea-party relations and value authenticity. One key or cue to a reason to reconnect will be you owning your behaviours and not just blaming me like you have been. The truth is you have been grossly cruel and that needs to be acknowledged or I will assume reconciliation is not happening.

God has given me the strength to go on with my own life, irregardless. The Hurting Moms online support group has helped.

Life is never so hard it is impossible to live, never so easy that its actually easy.

It used to drive me crazy but it wasn't a long trip –ha– ha– when you chewed on ice cubes. It wrecks the enamel on teeth.

Do you remember when I refused to pay for anymore of your braces because you were lipping off to me. Why pay for a mouth that only ever curses and disrespects me. It was not applauded by the dental office, but the down payment had been paid and these days no one disciplines a child anymore so they could eat dirt as far as I was concerned. This was my life and my problem child and I handled it to suit me. And then your dad was mad and paid a few instalments.

I cut off your cellphone for the same reason; they were always used to beak off and text spam me rudely. I excused myself from an orientation day on a new job to cut off your cell service in mid stream. Then your dad was on my case and I told him; "you want to be involved? Tell your demon spawn to smarten up." Ooooh, that wasn't a good thing to say. If it matters what we think it matters what we say." I have repented many times over and still do— for saying the wrong things out loud. No wonder the Bible says; "we take every thought captive and make it give up and obey Christ." 2 Corinthians 10:5 (NIV) and Proverbs 18:21 "The tongue has the power of life and death." (NIV).

It is awful to not be able to embrace people. This social distancing is wrecking lives designed to be connected. Automobile accidents have killed more people than covid and no one was ever ordered to stop driving except for a guilty drunk driver.

There was a guy who killed one of a set of twin males somewhere down east and he got away with it because he wasn't "drunk driving," he was "sleep driving." What next! "Uh, ossifer, I was actually just sleep-drunking..." Honestly!

Anyway, I had better go before they write a country song about me— The Rambler." I can see it now. Well as long as I get paid royalties.

Love, Mom

"Trauma teaches you to close your heart and armour up. Healing teaches you to open your heart and boundary up." –Unknown

May 10th, 2020

Dear Riley;

Happy Mother's Day to me, cuz goodness knows that worked out well. Yes, I still struggle with bitterness and against human nature in general. You can't change what you don't acknowledge.

It is a total act of forgiveness to even be writing this journal. I am walking in rueful forgiveness.

Your Dad once expressed doubt over your paternity and I shut him up good: "anytime you want to run a blood test, go for it. There won't be any surprises." Do you remember the side profile pics I took of you and your Dad in La Loche on Canada Day of...2011? There's your blood test results.

He cheated death a few times before he died, had more lives than a cat did, it seemed.

When you, your sister and I could not decide on a movie we threw some VHS choices into a pillowcase, shook them and then drew on out. There is a pillowcase in with your stuff.

Hopefully you will forgive me for the missing locks of hair. After the last bout of pain you caused me I had to do something to help myself and the hair went into the earth along with a tooth.

My prayer is that one day, very soon, you will get the mental health help you need. I suspect Antisocial Personality Disorder to name one, Conduct Disorder, and Oppositional Defiance Disorder for another. You can't change what you don't acknowledge and knowledge is power. Definition is a big part of problem solving too.

Some say labelling is disabling. Sometimes, I suppose it is, like when people pass judgment or when someone sits in meetings calling themselves an alcoholic over and over long after they have quit. What is wrong with placing an ex in front of the word if it is past tense.

Looking at my life one might say "x" is my favourite letter of the alphabet. Ha ha. No. I always played for keeps, the men I have known did not.

I asked a woman who had been married 60 years what her secret was. She was a flaming Narcissist, but she said without hesitation; "pick a good one in the first place." That was my flaw—I had a broken picker. So now I just don't anymore.

Love, Mom

_____

_____

_____

"If the shoe fits, wear it." –Unknown

"If the shoe fits get it on sale in every colour, then wear it with matching outfits." –Me.

May 17th, 2020

Dear Riley;

Today is the anniversary of my wedding to what's-his-drip in B.C. Seventeen years ago I walked up the aisle too stressed out to enjoy my overdone wedding and unhappy from the get-go. The pictures–with his face blacked out still scream Easter Parade on steroids. The pastel colours that were passe' even then plus the orange church carpet...yikes.

The windstorm with the lush green lawn is a controversy, not to mention nuisance. I can't get my yard work done. Jeepers, was I always a yard Nazi?

You know you were born to be an artist before anything else right? Art brings me feeling closer to you.

I hope the boxed up stuff of yours doesn't radically set you off onto a vendetta bender again. Your tirades are brutal and I have a right to be safe.

Today I made a list in my prayer journal about all the unresolved stuff in my life and gave it to God. You were the first item.

Sometimes I wish you were dead so you would stop causing relentless pain. Sometimes I am convinced losing a kid to rebellion is worse than a fatal crash. Because like this, the rusty fork just keeps dragging through my nerves. There is something to be said for ripping the duct tape off your skin quickly. Getting it over with.

Love, Mom

_____

_____

_____

"I will give back to her the vineyards she had and make Trouble Valley a door of hope." Hosea 2:15 (GNB)

May 12th, 2020

Dear Riley;

Man I have been waiting a long time for that promise up there. All your life.

I want to buy a ton of buttons to put in with your stuff to jog your memories of the days when we made "button pictures" together. The world is opening up again soon, maybe I can clean out a thrift store of their button supply.

The trouble is, I think in the first two years of your life I made the biggest mistake parenting. We did everything together and my life was all about you. Then when your colicky little sister came along with part of her spine fused and not separating so she could grow, you were rudely bumped off the lap and never got over it.

The movie; Lost Girls on Netflicks, reminded me of us, and the mother was totally me. I alternated between thinking you were like the missing girl or similar to the second oldest daughter. Not that you are a prostitute or a drug addict, but the addiction to anger and raging is very much still an addiction.

I have made up my mind I am no longer asking anyone twice for anything. Be it a job or whatever. Too much of my time has been wasted on complete wastes, and I am done. Someone told me once upon meeting a man; "if you don't feel like a queen in the first five minutes, walk away. It doesn't get better after that." That could apply to other things.

The language of language is changing. How often I have said "we just don't speak the same English," about someone I don't jive with.

I also remembered some more senior swears: "I've got myself all in a dither," (disoriented, basically) and "I've got my dander up/hackles raised," meaning my instincts are telling me somethings wrong. Then there's "—by grimeny!" Same as by golly, and the disjointed; "well I'll be go to hell."

When I was a teenager we said "psych!" instead of just kidding, and "enk! WRONG!" for telling someone they had a wrong answer. Or we added the word NOT to the end of a sarcastic statement. "enk! WRONG!"

It still boggles the mind how a wrong relationship can screw up your life or how early trauma over a bad breakup can actually cause P.T.S.D. Association has been a real problem in my life in general. I attract a-holes and seem to be drawn to them, and you can't rule them out in the workplace if you have to work which I do...

At school they outlawed bullying, at work they just call it upper management. Ha ha.

Anyway, I live in pain because of what our relationship is and if God didn't carry me I would be a grease stain on the sidewalk or a puddle in the gutter. I told Him I am fine if there are only ever one set of footprints in the sand—be they His and not mine. Amen.

Love, Mom

"When people ask, "what do you do?" Answer: "Whatever it takes."-Unknown

May 13th, 2020

Dear Riley;

Rachel said not to bother with the buttons because you wouldn't keep them. I told her not to give out my address or particulars of any kind, not to relay messages or to be a mule to ferry back any stuff. She said she wouldn't. The problem is Rachel is loyal to a fault.

Grandpa K said, "go ahead, give her all the baby books and then she will see how much you loved her."

I have nightmares about you in trouble with the law making the headlines and myself hiding from the media. Then I wake up and the nightmare continues, my own daughter hates me. And quite honestly, sometimes I hate my own daughter.

It was good to get that stuff out of my house. Like the lid of the coffin creaking shut slowly instead of being locked in the open position.

Here they pile such a big pile of clay-like dirt on top of a fresh burial-are they afraid of someone resurfacing? Well, believers of Jesus will anyway so...

You have my "first take no crap" policy in your personality. Just don't do it as a victim, or Very Insecure Child Trapped in Muck. Don't ask "why?" because the question "why" is the lingo of the victim mentality. On the other hand, ironically, the person asking the questions has all the control of the conversation, unlike a victim.

It's is ironic also, that playing the role of a victim is an attempt to gain control of the situation, so why not just be in control of oneself in the first place.

anyway, I am off on a tangent again. Did you know there is a place called Tangent in Alberta?

You used to tell people: "don't talk to me that way." I say let 'em talk any old way they want—just walk away.

Love, Mom

_____

_____

_____

"Even if you are on the right track, you will get run over if you just sit there."—On a poster in the school janitors office where I went to elementary and junior high school.

May 14th, 2020

Dear Riley;

I wonder if life comes with a manure quota and if so, shouldn't mine be full by now. Feels as if I have lived largely as a human outhouse, catching everybody's crap. But that's victim thinking and one should just be grateful Jesus made a way for us. Nothing about His life or death was fair, and that injustice He suffered enables me to trade burdens with Him; "for my yoke is easy and my burden is light."

Mostly I don't think like a helpless person anymore, I just pray you reconnect to God before the great eternal curtain closes for good. And that the never ending mental funeral for you will be over.

Yesterday the world opened up again, for better or forget it. The oil economy wasn't even recovered yet when this virus hit but people turned to God more than ever.

In my boredom I decorated my little red car to look like a giant ladybug since it is red and small. If you were here we could do it together, like when we decorated the hedge for S's birthday and the police stopped and asked us what we were doing. Ha ha, that was funny. If we had bolted they would have known we were guilty but we just turned and said no we hadn't seen "a tall guy running through here."

When I pray for you or anyone to become a believer in Jesus I don't ask for you to become a "Churchian" that becomes a pithy, pious, self-righteous jackass who looks down their nose at others. There are enough Pharisees already. I do hope you lose the spirit of pride and tremendous cultural arrogance which God can't negotiate. Us Germans have a lot of pride and where there is pride there is strife, the Bible says. Pride got Lucifer kicked out of heaven and demoted to evil.

It freaks me out when I can't picture you anymore or go through periods where I can't remember your childhood much. I don't know if that is trauma or unforgiveness talking.

Almighty God, I ask for the ability to forgive and remember the right things, and to be able to forget the negatives which serve no purpose other than for telling my story. I surrender my mind to you for healing, victory, freedom, and joy in the midst of sorrow. Amen.

Love, Mom

"If God brings you to it He will bring you through it."—Unknown

May 15th, 2020

Dear Riley;

Relinquishing control is not your thing nor mine, but we have to learn to let go and let God. Especially with worry and anxiety. I have to place you in His care and leave you there. God held you first and He holds you again and he knows how to keep holding you. I need to keep my mitts off.

Big Daddy doesn't need my help to heal you, but He sometimes takes His kids to work with Him and let them help. So I am confused sometimes as to when to let go and when to "help," the situation by continual prayer. I find myself nagging God and acting like I think He is behind in his work.

There are so many items awaiting His response I feel as if EVERYTHING I ever asked for is on hold. Our relationship is a Gideon/Lazarus/Ezekiel's bones situation; less resources=more God, late is not too late and bare bones can be fleshed out again and given life. Trouble is patience is a fruit of the spirit and I seem to be a spiritual vegetarian...Love, Mom

"You can't put a crown on a clown and expect a king."-Unknown

"Don't blame a clown for being a clown, ask yourself why you keep going to the circus."-Unknown

"Maturity is learning to walk away from people and situations that threaten your peace of mind, self-respect, values, morals, or self-worth."-Unknown

May 16th, 2020

Dear Riley;

You used to come running when I picked you up from daycare. I miss those days when I remember them. Most days my mind blanks out your memories.

Everyone is selling masks now, and I want one that says give me all your money, lol. I'll bet a ski mask will get you to the front of the line faster.

Work in this no-oil/virus riddled economy is beyond slow. You need that ski mask or a mini skirt to survive this economy and I'd get them mixed up I bet.

Not being allowed to love someone you love is pure agony. A piece of hell really.

My prayer today is that you would have a Damascus Road Epiphany where you will see yourself through God's eyes. I pray He turns my little Saul into... Paulette.

Whenever I think there is a person that is hopeless I think about Saul in the Bible and remember no one is beyond grace. If God can reach a serial-killer (which is how I have always see Saul before his conversion and he was part of the crowd that stoned Stephen) then He can reach anybody.

Oddly too how the scriptures never mention Saul/Paul going to jail until he was preaching about Jesus and then he was always in jail. Some televangelist joked about how Paul would have called ahead of each speaking engagement and asked if the jails had vacancy.

My point, and I do have one...there goes the theory that everything works well if you are a good person and only bad things happen to evil people. HAH. As if.

There's a lame joke about how two boys in a christian youth group were both after the same girl, named Grace. The one boy wins her over and the jilted one sends him a note; "My Grace is sufficient for thee." The other one responds with; "God resists the proud but gives Grace to the humble." Now you see what I had to endure in my youth group days, lol. Good thing no one said; "but to each of us Grace has been given..."

Incest joke; "how did the Mennonite find his sister in the corn field?"

Answer; "pretty good."

Yuck! I remember you once telling me Aboriginals
didn't have that problem...

Love, Mom

_____

_____

_____

May 17th, 2020

Loss

There is a death

no coffins bear

The end of life

sight doesn't share.

Unfulfilled dreams

A wish deferred

The end of hope

That no one heard.

A friendship[gone

A love once strong

To grieve an end

A pain too long.

No measured loss

When living part

A life gone south

Still breaks you heart.

To end a thing

Is sad you see

Sometimes events

Near buried me.

By Mom

_____

_____

_____

"In peace I will lie down and sleep, for you alone, Lord, make me dwell in safety." Psalm 4:8 (NIV)

May 18th, 2020

Dear Riley;

Scripture for the insomniac. You inherited mine and so did Rachel.

I try not to do this often but I looked in the bathroom mirror today and had the usual self-criticism and general "I hate my body," experience. The God asked me if I would rather not have had children, and I answered no, I would keep my children and altered body, thank you. But I have regretted having reproducing and He understands, He has had the same feelings. Genesis 6:6.

I have zero sympathy for bored married men. A woman gives all of herself to a relationship and a man never quite has to evidently. They are guaranteed orgasm if they are healthy, we are not wired to be satisfied so easily and then they traumatize her body with their babies and THEY get bored?! Do you know how many ceiling tiles I have counted in my lifetime? Lol. Enough to wallpaper a large ballroom, no pun intended. Hee hee.

There is such peace again about you, that God's got this and no matter if we ever reconnect, we are covered by His wings. That means He has feathers and can relate to prow wow dancers.

The world reopening again feels surreal. Or it is P.T.S.D. talking. That is one of its special effects. Ha ha. Just once I would like my jaw to hang because of some wonderful incident.

I went Charlie Sheen on the yard again. Those garden boxes that look like caskets without lids have to go, I have permission from the landlord. They bug me. I tried to give them away on kijiji but no one would take them, so now its sledge hammer time.

It's funny how the heart has no brains. No matter how many times I have said I am done with men I will not ever completely shut that door. In this town you have to be careful though, it is quite toxic and a question equals a commitment rather than a mere conversation. They take things waaaaay too seriously here.

Soon I will be busking at the farmers markets because the economy sucks ostrich eggs on a stick. It instrumental music—maybe just mental, ha ha; so it should be allowed. I am not spitting on anybody—say it don't spray it has taken on a whole new meaning.

Love, Mom

"Flowers don't worry about how they are going to bloom. They just open up and turn toward the light and that makes them beautiful." -Jim Carey.

May 19th, 2020

Dear Riley;

There are things that affected you life that were beyond my control, like how you were trapped next to the debris of two other fetuses that had passed away in-utero. You were born three weeks premature and got whisked away for the first four hours for not breathing right. Back then I don't think they knew how damaging it could be, plus being the sole survivor of the pregnancy. It had to have affected you negatively.

The act of blaming however, is a toxic behaviour along with fault finding and accusing. So I try not to go there, it's counter productive. But maybe it is a future lawsuit to hold people responsible and make sure it doesn't happen to others, because studies have been done since on how the first four hours after birth are crucial to bonding time between mom and baby.

Well this is probably repetitious, and repetition is the language of trauma and religion, lol. The good news is God won't let anything happen to you that He can't or won't heal. Sometimes He waits to be asked. But one of my favourite verses is John 8:36 (NIV) "So if the Son sets you free you shall be free indeed."

Today I went Martha Stewart on the flowerbed and put Marigolds and Irises together and then set a white wire lounge chair in it with pink throw pillows on it. It looks so amazing, and it's not bragging if its true. Once the foliage fleshes out it will look even better.

I hope you are doing well and getting the therapy you need, the healing and the restoration.

Love, Mom

"Your most effective ministry will come out of your deepest hurts."–Rick Warren

"Other people are going to find healing in your wounds."–Rick Warren

May 20th, 2020

Dear Riley;

You look just like Pocahontas, I tell everyone that. Disneyland would hire you, lol.

When you go through the boxes of stuff I am sending with Rachel I hope you have an open mind about the items included that reminded me of your father. Of course the danger of keeping an open mind is your brains could fall out, ha ha.

You know these days sometimes pillars in the community are really just piles of baloney. Did you know it was church leaders that killed Jesus? Matthew 27:1-2 (KJV) "when the morning was come, all the chief priests and elders of the people took counsel against Jesus to put him to death..." So for as long as time has existed, people haven't been who they claimed to be.

I when I think about my life and get overwhelmed at the huge injustices I have suffered, I read Corrie Ten Boom's book; "The Hiding Place," or watch "The Making Of A Murderer," on Netflicks. Or I just plain recall the story of Jesus who chose to suffer injustice so He could save me. There was nothing fair about being born to die. Injustice there has done me a huge favour.

I try not to hold people against God either. Looking at the hypocrisy I have known alone is enough to turn a believer into an atheist. God is still good.

It's time for the dog to walk me again and don't think I don't appreciate his dedication to zig zagging around me like I am his cow to herd. Thaaaaaaanks dude.

Love, Mom

_____

_____

_____

"If you break someone and they still wish you the best, you've lost the greatest thing for you."—Unknown

May 27th, 2020

Dear Riley;

Today your childhood memorabilia was delivered and your sister said it was uneventful. My phone has been extra noisy today with email sounds but then when I look there is nothing. The old account was settled long ago you might say. When I broke my phone last December everything had to be reset. Now you have no access to any of my contact information.

Poor Rachel, she so badly wants to be from a cohesive family and it shows on her. This isn't what she signed up for; the fight she was raised in between you and I has simply continued, nay, escalated to flat out you stalking me on Instagram and committing hate crimes by sending harassing emails; "You white people all look like cottage cheese," and "I wish you were dead you skank," blah blah etcetera. I think that constitutes as a hate crime.

I have even prayed some hard petitions for you that if it is necessary for your journey back to sanity that you would get into trouble with the law. "Lord if she isn't going to stop on her own, (the hateful, harassing behaviours) let her do it to the wrong person once and get charged. Not that I am "the right person" to do this to; send blood curdling emails of hatred from my own daughter. I would even consider testifying against you if I knew about an incident and thought it would do any good in the long run.

A year ago I applied for a restraining order but the R.C.M.P. And Calgary City Police are two forces that usually don't work together. Not that I couldn't or wouldn't drive to the city and file a complaint if the circumstance called for it.

Today I conclude my prayer with; "stop her Lord. Do whatever it takes."

Tough love,

Mom

_____

_____

_____

"Don't make someone your priority who has only made you an option."–Unknown

"Even the strongest feelings expire when ignored and taken for granted."–Unknown

May 22nd, 2020

Dear Riley;

God is with me in the pain you are causing. "Even if I go through the deepest darkness, I will not be afraid, Lord, for you are with me. Your shepherd's rod and staff protect me." Psalm 23:4(GNB).

I am learning over and over again that God is all I need and God is enough, people and things are just a bonus. I understand Gethsemane, the lonesome valley; Hagar in the wilderness. Alone with God is alone with everything you need.

Rachel only lasted four months without me because of listening to her father's fables. She has been back with me ever since but I am experiencing God is enough.

I sent your Bible back, I hope you can't bring yourself to throw it away or pass it on. When you sent it back to me I went to erase your name to make it non personalized so I could pass it along as a gift and God said; "what are you doing?! She is going to need it." So I kept it and then returned it along with all the silver rings you gave back to Rachel to be hurtful. We used to have a thing where you and I liked each other's birthstones better than our own. That's the only reason I bought you Amethysts and myself pearls. Then I found a dark pearl and thought how perfect for you aboriginal ancestry. But the things I did for you got swept under the tide of rage you insist on.

"So also will be the word that I speak—it will not fail to do what I plan, it will do everything I sent it to do." Isaiah 55:11(GNB). There is a reason I pray Ezekiel 37:4-6 over us; the dry bones becoming flesh again. With God, it ain't over 'til it's over, and human "over," is not the same as His. I grew up with the saying; "it ain't over 'til the fat lady sings."

Lord, don't let Riley throw out her Bible. Don't let her destroy your word, cause her to be drawn to it instead. In Jesus Name, Amen.

Love, Mom

_____

_____

_____

"The lord works righteousness and justice for all the oppressed." Psalm 103:6 (NIV)

"For I will restore health to you and heal you of your wounds, says the Lord, because they called you an outcast saying: 'this is Zion; No one seeks her.'" Jeremiah 30:17 (NIV).

May 23rd, 2020

Dear Riley;

Now I am up to writing about the first week of your life in the book; "Growing Up Men," where we spent a week in the hospital. You were sluggish, jaundiced and not breastfeeding well. All you wanted to do is sleep and the face you made at the nurses when they woke you up was so like your father. It was funny; a tiny infant that already knew how to glare.

When you were a month old I gave up breastfeeding and stuck you on the bottle. I felt terrible about it. Then as a teenager, you returned to it. I like to think bringing home a four pack of coolers and a package of cigarettes for you and Rachel to legitimately try rather some somebody's home cooked deal. It seemed to teach you both responsibility around those things and now neither of you drinks and drives nor leaves their drink unattended, but you drink.

It's good that you are blocked from sending your barrage of insults to my email account. That is out and out criminal behaviour. You are responsible for yourself and your actions, no matter how much you have convinced yourself that you are a justified victim.

The only real victims of life are dead people. The rest make choices about their experiences.

Those who sow wind will reap a storm, and boy, do I see clouds gathering for you.

Tough love,

Mom

_____

_____

_____

"Where God sees a scar He creates a star."-Robert Schuller, senior.

"I have heard your prayer and seen your tears, I will heal you." 2nd Kings 20:5 (NIV).

May 24th, 2020

Dear Riley;

Just because I forgive and am at peace doesn't mean facts fade from view. And it doesn't mean I stop praying tough prayers for you.

You were a baby that didn't feed well, then a toddler that displayed symptoms of pica disease; eating paper rather ravenously. Then when I urged you to eat your food up so we could move onto the next thing you threw the dish on the floor. When you finished a bottle and if we were walking outside you chucked it into traffic.

One doctor said Asperger's Syndrome, another said Autism. I saw signs of Oppositional Defiance Disorder, and your overly dramatic step Grandmother said Bipolar Disorder. At the very least, there were signs of Neurosis. Finally after a six week stay in the hospital for kids with mental health issues, they came up with Anxiety and how you needed to be part of a discussion in the discipline at home. Uh huh. Yup. Right. I was sooo glad someone paid that doctor besides me. With a system like that who needs problems?! and my point is, I tried hard to get you help. Yet it seems like anything great ever accomplished was performed by someone with a mental illness. Albert Einstein was dyslexic; Winston Churchill was Bipolar, Lady Diana had Borderline Personality Disorder. The so-called most healthy people who think they have their manure in a mass/poop in a group can't see their own delusions of grandiosity. If you think there is nothing wrong with you then that's your something wrong with you.

The best church I ever attended was the psychiatric hospital. Everyone for the most part was kind and stuck together—we knew we were all the same. No one put on any airs but try and walk into a certain church here and it reeks with the sh—that doesn't stink. If you know what I mean.

A counsellor once told me; "it is your thoughts around the problem that is worse than the problem itself."

You are a lot like me, and I am smiling because there is nothing you can do about it; 51 percent sweetheart, 49 percent something else...don't anyone push their luck.

Love, Mom

_____

_____

_____

"It's better to be an old man's darling than a young man's slave."–Your K grandparents

"Some people are brought together in the devil's wheelbarrow."–Your K grandparents

May 25th, 2020

Dear Riley;

I hope when I share my testimony if it is on somethingtube it won't trigger you into another vendetta bender. I will pray much about it. Nothing happens in my life without much sprechting much with God.

The devil has no chance against a mother's prayers, but I get so impatient. I just want you to get the help you need and get better.

It is awful waiting to see what ugly thing you will do next in your great venom spewing racket. It used to rotate on a 90 day cycle so there must be a Bipolar Disorder there.

In my darkest moments I have told myself a little bit of racism would have saved me a ton of grief. But mostly I find aboriginal people beautiful. Unresolved grief twists you all up in the game.

In my darkest minute, I say to myself; well, Mary had a kid with God and I guess I had one from the devil. It would unhinge the perfect jaw of every long faced legalist and self righteous grunt if they knew. Oh friggen well. This is my story to tell.

By now you must be in line to be the next prime minister with all your fancy book learnin.' Lol.

Love Mom

_____

_____

_____

"Sometimes God blesses us not in what He gives us, but what He takes away." –Unknown

"God knows how to give you back what the enemy convinced you that you lost." –Unknown

May 26th, 2020

Dear Riley;

Rachel's best friend C looks like you and she is actually part aboriginal. So it is rather therapeutic to see them together, as if our family is still intact. I'll take what I can get.

My car is now converted to look like a giant ladybug. Someone said "hey the dots don't look right." I said; "well, it's been drinking." Out of boredom during the shutdown I ordered peel and stick eyelashes to place above and below the headlights. The dots nicely cover body damage and help me to decide where the next one goes. Ha ha.

The garish thoughts of dread around you are back and I can't explain them. A long faced legalist would judge me and say it is unforgiveness. I say not actually. More like P.T.S.D. effects. I feel as though I am waiting for a phone call with bad news or a bad news report about something you have done. So I pray once more for peace like Jimmy Swaggert's river.

A week ago I had a wedding proposal from a guy I just met. He said the three words every woman loves to wants to hear; "I have money." Ha ha. Then he proceeded to try and swallow up my life with a barrage of texts and phone calls until I said no and blocked him. Now we are not even friends.

Did you graduate from another level of social work this year, I wonder.

Well, I am exhausted as per usual.

Gotta go napping.

Love, Mom

_____

_____

_____

"If your absence doesn't bother them your presence doesn't matter to them in the first place."–Unknown

"Those who matter won't mind and those who mind don't matter."–Unknown

May 27th, 2020

Dear Riley;

I think the quote directly above refers to toxic people that are always offended over something.

The world is still very much locked up behind masks and leery proximity. The virus has also provided an excuse for rudeness and new strange rules that really have nothing to do with the disease. But let's face it, negativity sells and so does fear-mongering. The planet is upholstered in mindless sheep and solar-powered bobble heads that need to be told what to think next, how to think it and when.

Today the gospel of OCD was alive and well. I picked at the yard some more, it has to be perfect. All three of us have symptoms of OCD.

You called me, above all things, a narcissist and if it is true it is hereditary. I am actually an Empath that can read most people like a Dick and Jane reader. Us empaths often fall prey to a narcissist. Eat that.

I pray everyday God puts an end to the strife between us. Then there are days when I cannot even pray and I panic until I realize "poor old God" doesn't actually need my help and Jesus "ever lives to make intercession for them."

How else are any of us here but for the grace of God and the prayers of Jesus?

Love, Mom

_____

_____

_____

"Trauma: a reaction that happens when the body goes through more internal and external changes than it can handle."—Unknown

May 28th, 2020

Dear Riley;

That was me on December 15th, 2019. Looking back now I do not know how I made it to my bed from the kitchen so drunk. Maybe Angelo dragged me. I said when he came to house sit there was a trail of broken glass and blood from the kitchen sink to the master bedroom and I had no open cuts when I got to the hospital and I bled like a speared monkeys uncle from just the I.V. insertion so it beats me what exactly happened. The officer's paperwork only mentioned the pills all over the counter-top.

I am staring blankly at the page...not a good indication that the coffee has kicked in...need to shed that habit anyway. Caffeine is an addiction and if you don't think so try cutting it off cold turkey. By day three you will have a screaming headache. That's withdrawal.

The world continues to feel surreal after the "planned-demic." I don't think much of anything goes on in the world that isn't manipulated by the government. I also think there is room for all of us and our individual opinions or we wouldn't all be here. Rachel and I do not agree on vaccinations and stuff like that. I have even had threatening things said to me on social media when I was on it because of my wrong opinions. Oh well. If the planet can't hold us all there's a problem. I let people think what they want; it's called live and let live.

It's equally disappointing how "born again christians" have lapped up social media as a good thing. Not that the saintliest of "holy-molies," as I call self-righteous Churchians, has any problem whatsoever with gossip. And social media is a gossip tool so hence my take it is a tool of the devil as was the internet before that which enabled people to find lost lovers and cheat and access other evil. But don't anyone stop and think for yourselves. Oh no. Because that might require change.

Anyway the meticulous yard work is a distraction from emotional pain. I forgot there is a few bald patches that need grass seed so I will go buy some. The landlord loves me. The landlord had better love me, lol.

The coffin boxes are gone from the yard with the help from the neighbour and his chain saw. There is still the dilapidated shed in the corner and the brush pile in the adjacent corner and this place is cleaned up. Yay me.

Listening to the clock ticking...still not a sign of caffeine or any steam for the dream. Igh carumba.

There is such a peace about you today, no matter what happens. I love those days. Thank you Lord. Amen.

Love, Mom

"I just wanna be the just who live by faith, the righteous who don't beg bread and the sheep who hear his voice." —Me

May 29th, 2020

Dear Riley;

That is not to be confused with my wanting to be a mindless sheep. Nope.

Did I ever tell you your great grandfather fought in the second world war? Kind of. He fought against it period. They shipped him to a Conscientious Objectors Camp because he didn't want to commit murder. He was my person, such a cool cat.

Church has resonated in my mind as a place where evil people conglomerate to try and fix their evilness and just end up as evil people with a religion. I have been supremely sh—on in this religious town, and I can get that experience as someone people love to hate anywhere I don't need it again in church.

You cannot hold people against God, however, you have to separate the sheep from the goats with God's help and wisdom; "show me who you want in my life and vice versa, Lord."

I do hope/pray/wish you and Rachel will become close to God and look after your spiritual selves, cuz that's where it's at.

It's getting harder and harder to write. I guess it is a good thing-getting emptied of grief over you. If that's what it is.

The thing is, you don't just burn a bridge, you bomb it. Parents of dead children don't understand losing a child to rebellion; "at least she can come back," or "she might come back." I wonder if the finality of death is better than the long good bye in the long run. There is something to be said for ripping that duct tape off the planter's wart quickly.

Love and weariness,

Mom

_____

_____

_____

"Nothing happens until the pain of remaining the same outweighs the pain of change." -Arthur Burt

May 30th, 2020

Dear Riley;

You remember our Seventh Day Adventist Days, yes? I would not ever want to go back to being religious but I think I will return to Sabbath Keeping. Life was better when I did.

Did you know clumsiness is an extreme gene in the family? So I asked your sister yesterday if you are clumsy because I couldn't remember. She was always a klutz. I would hear a racket and then she would announce; "nuthin's broke." It was funny.

What I recall is for your entire life, your weight has been up and down.

It remains a pretty grim economy out there, I can't even get work from the last place to get work from.

Your Aunt M1 is telling me what to do right now. Some things never change, the youngster trying to be the older sibling.

I watched Lost Girls again today. I can so relate to Mari Gilbert, the Mom.

Today was another day for crappy wind storms and rain. The second in a row. I feel it goes along with everything else in life anymore. It's hard to keep spirits up.

Did you ever get into ceramics. Man they are addictive. I saw a mug once that said "Polish Mug," and the handle was on the inside.

While I was in the "Puzzle Palace" I was in my full glory in arts class and ceramics. But they wouldn't let me take my "Nobody's Prefect" mug home. The staff was constantly testing us to see if we would detonate under pressure and I never did. I learned to nod and smile and say; "oh okay," a lot because I wanted outta there, crafts and hot tubs or not. It's called eat sh— and smile, a skill I always lacked!

Love, Mom

_____

_____

_____

"God has the power to turn your test into a testimony. Allow Him to finish your story." -Unknown

"The righteous person may have many troubles, but the Lord delivers him from them all." Psalm 34:19 (NIV).

Dear Riley;

I wish I had sat cross legged on the floor more and played with you instead of being so riddled with O.C.D. and busy cleaning. I wish I had given you affection every time you needed it, especially after discipline.

Amazing things happen with the phase "God, I willing..." Just a few days ago I said I was willing to forgive men and then when I punted a guy I wasn't angry anymore than when I felt was warranted. Forgiveness and release are practically the same word.

Then afterward I burned a bunch of brush of stuff in the yard- brush from previous tenants mostly. I am a lousy pyromaniac and even lousier arsonist but some gas helped. Singed my wig really well too.

I can still hear the wind howling around the house like Laura Ingalls commercial. Frig I hate wind.

I pray you get the help you need soon. You cannot differentiate between a lie and the truth. A symptom of a type of Bipolar Disorder, and there are 7.

Tomorrow I have to run into R----again. Your favourite town, mine too. An angry lynch mob looking for an excuse and the buy and sell site on social media is the gallows. I always found that to be a brown town. Censorship...

I pray for the faith to have the faith to pray a little more...and then get answers. I am grateful when I think of all the prayers I never had to pray because God already blessed me. And He is not my employee seeking to please me, I should serve Him. Yet He came to seek and save, with an attitude of "can I get that for you?" Our God who made the universe asks how He can serve me?! It makes me cry, because only once in a while I seek to serve him rather than myself...but there is hope.

Love, Mom

"The Lord makes firm the steps of the one who delights in Him." Psalm 37:23 (NIV)

"Do the best you can until you know better. Then when you know better, do better."—Maya Angelou

June 1st, 2020

Dear Riley;

There sure isn't much work in this town other than pumping gas and working the cash register, although I am sure no one calls the jobs that anymore. Waitresses are now servers, gas pumpers are attendants, and cashiers are either that or customer service representatives. Slavery was done away with by changing its name to employment.

Most people here are friendly and kind, except the "christians." Those you have to watch out for. Churchians, really, is a better name for those. There's a lot of churchianity here.

It is a chore to have to go to R------- and feel the oppression as thick as goat cheese in the air. I regret ever moving us there but what can I possibly do about it now? Zippy.

Where you and Rachel get your ability to save money from I will never understand. I want a blood test, ha ha.

Now there are only pictures of you in a few family photos on the wall. That is all I have left.

Well the lawn mower has a blunt blade and so does my axe so its time to take them in to be sharpened. It's no surprise, the way I have been hacking away at the jungle, cleaning up behind other people. See? You're not the only one with an axe to grind. Ha ha.

The people who sharpen blunt objects run their business out of a plastic recipe card box and take cash or cheque only. I love it.

So it is beautiful out here, but lots of work. My arms ache like a country song.

Love, Mom

_____

_____

_____

"You have within you, right now, everything you need to deal with whatever the world can throw at you."—Unknown

"But you belong to God, my children, and have defeated the false prophets, because the Spirit who is in you is more powerful than the spirit in those who belong to the world." 1 John 4:4 (GNB).

June 2nd, 2020

Dear Riley;

Sometimes I think stonewalling is a man's greatest skill set in conflict and I don't mean masonry. But once again, I have told God I am willing to be willing to forgive all men. And most of all the anger and bitterness is gone.

Today I got the brush pile down to the ground. The yard work is done except for regular maintenance. It is gorgeous—and it isn't bragging if its true.

Four or five years ago Rachel moved out and I am still struggling with the empty nest syndrome.

Today I felt ragged enough to drink. Or smoke. Or something. I quit social drinking since the incident, however. About five and a half months ago. Yay me.

Life hurts. The trick is to give God the pain. My broken toe from dropping a glass table top on it, a dog bite from the weird mongrel in R——————, do not help. Although it is literal ouch to go with the emotional so I have a visual aide. I prefer to be numb but to get rid of it you have to feel pain.

It is amazing how many women I have heard say over a lifetime of running from psycho men myself; "I would rather have a physical blow than be emotionally abused." A support group leader summarized it well- she didn't negate it- "you can put your finger on a bruise, you know it's there and you can see it disappear over time, but emotional scars take longer." And unresolved wounds tend to cloud our vision.

There is a line from the Gaither hymn; "I Will Serve Thee," and it goes like this: "heartaches broken pieces, ruined lives are why you died on Calvary." That is my spiritual insurance plan. I know He died for me and if only for me.

Okay well it is time to quit feeling sorry for myself and get on with the day. Experience, not suffering.

Love, Mom

"When you hurt the person who spends their nights praying for you and you think God won't compensate them, have fear." –Unknown

June 3rd, 2020

Dear Riley;

This journal is pink with black edges around the cover, printed with black designs. Very feminine. I find every woman whose femininity has been damaged hates the colour pink and I claim mine back. That part of spectrum is no longer the problem.

My tough prayers for you continue. Lately it's been for God to put a muzzle on your mouth so you don't speak evil. I also pray for protection from you. My own daughter. But I think you are sick.

I miss having two little girls to look after. At the time I was stressed and burdened, worried about babysitters and/or our next meal. Poverty robs. We could not afford to be allergic to peanut butter.

Today I saw an image of your face briefly before it went away.

The wind is so cold for June, it cuts off your ears and hands them to you. I practically had to ride my push mower to keep it from blowing away. Ha ha.

My home is Fort Knox; locked gates and signs claiming security cameras are present. Angelo, the big black dog you met once, is not enough to keep the wandering souls out. Only my house was targeted by "the chicken man," as I call him, no one else on the block. He seems harmless but mentally ill, the guy that wonders into my yard and tries to sell me eggs.

Did you know the human body starts healing the moment its injured? I like to think that is true for all of us; spirit, mind, body.

I actually pray against grandchildren until things are resolved between us. What a place to be in, to not want grand babies.

When my own stinking thinking gets to be too much I turn to God and the Book-Intended-Before-Losses-Erupted. (Bible).

"No one has ever seen or heard of a God like you, who does such deeds for those who put their hope in him." Isaiah 64:4 (GNB)

Love, Mom

_____

_____

_____

"Your relationships are meant to be your safe and happy place, not another battle you have to fight." Unknown and amen

June 4th, 2020

Dear Riley;

Where have all the grown men gone? Long time passing... lol. I wish I had given up on men twenty years ago. Right now I have more alone, than I ever did with any man. More sanity, peace, materially, etc.

The landlords came today it was so nice to visit with them and my dear little neighbour B. And it didn't hurt that they loved the condition of the house and yard.

Your favourite book to read when you were little was "Julie and the Puppy." I remember it had archaic language like "pram" for stroller and so on. But you loved it.

I am trying to prepare Rachel for her father's passing. He has brain cancer now and they aren't raising the covid isolation rules to let dying people have visitors. You have got to be kidding me. I don't know who I would hate enough to wish that lever of cruelty on them. Today it really hit me emotionally about what is happening to him, even though I see him as an absolute arse. He and I go back forever.

He had said some really cruel things to Rachel and she repeated them to me. I burst out with; "so he is going to be a PRICK to his last breath?!" She said, "mom! In what universe is that helpful?!"

Did I tell you mid life crisis has taken over and I am craving a boob job and a motorcycle? Lol.

Social isolation has numbed all our social skills, it seems. People don't even make eye contact at times. I had Covid and was socially distant before it was cool.

I know God has a thousand ways when I cannot see one, and I rely on Him now more than ever in my screwed up life. Especially now that our rickety planet seems to be wrapping up!

There's a t-shirt slogan in La Crete; "La Crete is not the end of the world, but you can see it from here." Lol. Well now it seems we are on the cusp of the end of time. And I say; "get; er done."

Love, Mom

_____

_____

_____

"The Lord will rescue me from every evil attack and will bring me safely into His heavenly kingdom. To Him be glory forever and ever. Amen." 2 Timothy 4:18 (NIV).

June 5th, 2020

Dear Riley;

Well today I had sawdust in my eyes where tears used to be and I took that to be a good sign. There were a few branches above my head on a maple tree out front that needed to go. Heaven forbid I put on one of my many pairs of safety glasses until after the fact. Then I trimmed the Ohio Buckeye that produces something like Hazelnuts. After that I let the day lapse into nothingness. Just a blah lack-luster day.

Never expect a relationship to make up for your past. It will ruin it. A preacher once said; "when it comes to people two halves make a quarter." And it's true. A lacking person with another deficit character does not create wholeness.

I think when the Book-Inspired-Before-Losses-Erupted talks about not being yoked unequally with people it doesn't mean a Muslim shouldn't marry a Mennonite. And it refers to more than romantic connections. I think it also means don't waste your time with "Lah-Dee-Dahs" that are too good for you. This town is chalk full of Spiritual Narcissists that think they are all that religiously. Well good for them—I'd hate to put that kind of pressure to perform on myself.

I went further in life than my mother did, technically, and you went further than I did. It's a good trend, dontcha think? Although your Gramma K made a career out of gardening, canning, cooking, and baking. I still call her sometimes and ask how to do things, but I have wrestled more demons than anyone I know.

Thanks to you I get too excited about bead work. Lol.

Its quiet and beautiful here, when the weather isn't under the weather. The crows cheerfully cackle in the trees so I hung up scary red eyed balloons to make like a new species had moved in so they all moved into the graveyard across the street from me. How fitting.

Joke; a man was diagnosed as terminally ill by his family doctor and given 6 months to live. "But doctor," the man protested. "I can't pay my medical bill off in such a short time!" So the doctor gave him six more months.

Love, Mom

"I used to think the worst thing in life was to end up alone, it's not. The worst thing in life is to end up with people who make you feel all alone." -Unknown

June 6th, 2020

Dear Riley;

I may not be completely innocent in the broken connections in my family tree-one cousin grew so tired of the yo-yo relationship I had with f--book that she quit talking to me altogether. But it is sad to come from such a huge family and still be so alone. So I have opted out of having a funeral ever and then those who didn't care can keep it right up. I read somewhere on the internet once that people bring more flowers to a grave than they gave that individual in real life because regrets outweigh appreciation. How sad is that.

Our family reunions which I haven't attended since I lived at home and was dragged to against my will, are awkward. Different church denominations sit with their peers and stare down their noses at the OTHERS. What is the point of that. That and the fact that my first love is married to my first cousin makes it hella weird for me. Your Great-Grandpa K's funeral was just another insult when they sat down right in front of me. Naturally me being me, had to make an insulting comment that burned his ass. I innocently asked if they were having their wedding there, knowing full well it would be at his church. In the Mennonite realm the woman follows the man. I was rewarded when he appeared annoyed. She resembles me when I am blonde except I never had such a wide wheel base. Perhaps she is his consolation prize, hand clapped over mouth. Yay me. Yay self-control too. Yup. Um hmm.

Honestly I wished I had given up on men a hundred years ago. If it were possible.

Communion is hard for me, I can clear the slate for five minutes but after that...see you are to forgive anyone that has an issue against you and vice versa or you are drinking damnation unto yourself. Hence why I may as well make change in the offering plate and spike the communion juice with Tabasco sauce. Now we really put that sh-- on everything. Hee hee. I offended the frick out of some churchians here making that joke. What a bunch of stiffs. As far as I am concerned that snake pit needs to be shut down for all kinds of reasons...a sex offender in leadership...another one— his buddy in song leadership...ya...clearly my jokes are THE PROBLEM. Oh Lord deliver me of bitterness, I am so tired of being the world's scapegoat when they already have one. Jesus.

I love this verse: "The Lord will grant that the enemies who rise up against you will be defeated before you. They will come at you from one direction, but flee from you in seven." Deuteronomy 28:7 (NIV).

I also love this: "...no weapon formed against you will prevail, and you will refute every tongue that accuses you. This is the heritage of the servants of the Lord, and this is their vindication from me, declares the Lord." Isaiah 54:17 (NIV).

Love, Mom

_____

_____

_____

"When someone tries to trigger you by insulting you or by doing or saying something that irritates you, take a deep breath and switch off your ego. Remember that if you are easily offended, you are easily manipulated." –Unknown

June 7th, 2020

Dear Riley;

Today I wrote a blog for mood-scope about being happy even when life hands us something other than what we ordered. My counselling course taught me "we must quit musterbating," or in plain English, we make ourselves miserable when we insist we will only be happy when we have our way.

Books were important part of our lives when you were little. We always had book orders we could not afford and I read bedtime stories until you no longer wanted them. It's a good thing I did not realize when the last one was.

I dumbed my class two licence down to a three quite unintentionally–I went to renew without a medical note and was told "you can't have the level 2 without it." I said "Great! I will just drop down," thinking it would be a class 5. "How about a 3?" she said. And walla! I became a trucker overnight. Most days I need a truck to go with my mouth anyway, lol.

Today the lawnmower quit, the vacuum already had and the car was going to if it didn't get an oil change. A country song.

It would appear as tough the wooing and winning of women is no more. Men are oblivious to the fact that women cost money. Life costs money. We grow up needing pantyhose, pads, hair gel, mousse, etcetera, and all they needed is the bra section of the free Sears catalogue. Ha ha.

Tomorrow is your birthday, although you should have been born July 2nd. One time we were so poor I went to the Salvation Army for groceries around your true due date and there sitting on the shelf was the perfect chocolate cake with pink roses in the frosting. As if God was telling me something...

I cringe sometimes when I think back to how I was raised with nothing, raised you with about as much, and now still, as a woman living alone, am broke-folk.

It isn't a crime nor a sin to be genuinely poor after you have done everything you possibly can to work. But try and tell that to a spoiled little rich b———— who came into this world with a gold cake server in his mouth. I wasn't born with a silver spoon it was more like a rusty fork. Lol. Love, Mom

"For Christ did not please himself. Instead, as the scripture says, "The insults of those who insult you have fallen on me."–Jesus (Romans 15:3 (GNB)

June 8th, 2020

Dear Riley;

Twenty three years ago I had you. Such a tiny human being. If I had seen the future then who knew what I would have done. You were the sole survivor of the triple pregnancy and I had triple the post-postpartum depression, a watermelon sized placenta and miles of umbilical cord. My body had prepared itself for triplets. I have tried not to tell that story often because the truth is crazier than fiction.

Rachel got some bad news today, her father is terminal with mere weeks left to live. Apparently by the sounds of things, he IS going to be a prick until his dying breath. And I am not swearing–that word is in the Bible.

Your fathers were both domestic abusers. It is hard to have anything but a hardened attitude toward such harsh men.

So much for a frothy, light, happy entry on your birthday. Like I said in the beginning of this book, I am not writing to please anyone, I am just writing to be. That and the cheapest form of therapy being a notebook and a pen.

Today I remembered the financial abuse from T, expecting me to work all kinds of graveyard shifts around other men but the question; "where are your rings?" He wanted me tagged like a dead moose while running around frantically supporting us both. He POUTED when I quit a job. Financial abuse doesn't feel much different than discovering you're being cheated on—maybe because you are being cheated out of what you need. Forcing a woman to work like a damn pimp with a hoe or blocking her from working when she wants to—its all financial abuse. If I have to do everything by myself, I think I'll just keep it up.

Lately I have been remembering your mouthiness growing up. Lord help the day you learned how to speak! Lately I have been praying; "shut her up Lord." Just shut her up. Maybe it is because I have been remembering the cruel words you have thrown.

It's hard to be someone who is hated as soon as I walk into a room. I told God; "my own kids have crucified me." He said; "ya I know the feeling."

When God speaks, it is so cool. It's like a thousand waterfalls but also a giant whisper, so loud yet so quiet at the same time—only Big Daddy (God) could pull that off. The neatest, most miraculous thing is when He laughs. That is water rippling over smooth stones in a brook. He used to tap me on the shoulder in the middle of the night—He has to talk to me in the night otherwise I am doing all the talking—and He'd say; "you awake?" I would say: "You are the Almighty and you had to ask?!" Ha ha.

I am going to buy the Sedona Sky ring to go with the set you have from a previous birthday and put it with the rest of your gifts.

Happy Birthday,

I love you,

—Mom

"Sleep doesn't help if it's your soul that's tired."-Unknown

June 9th, 2020

Dear Riley;

"It's a rainy day in June, the sky is grey, and I am blue." Line from an Alan Jackson song.

You and I used to bake together a lot. Then when Rachel got older she joined us.

The hurting Mom's support group has really helped, and that was two years ago.

When you raise children, you do your best by them and they turn out how they turn out. My parents would not walk across the street for me but I would take a bullet for them. Go figure.

The hermit life continues to look good in that cabin in the woods. With a satellite phone, radio and a generator of course. Ha ha.

July 5th is the 50th Wedding Anniversary of your K Grandparents, so we are giving them credit for time served. I am making a card that resembles the sign "Maximum 50."

I was raised that you grow up and get married. Some might argue that I never grew up so that should get me off the hook. Marriage was also very much upheld in my hometown. To the extreme where a wife of a man that raped all their daughters was praised for her love for him keeping the marriage together.

When I started a new relationship I had "the talk," with the individual, that my kids are trained to know the proper name for body parts and they are taught to talk so they will not keep the secret that someone molested them. I am surprised no one ran screaming just then. One guy that was short lived seemed to be trying to be grooming me to allow you and Rachel to be molested. He said; "for all you know they have been." I said very firmly; "if my kids tell me–and they will– that someone is touching them inappropriately, every guy I have ever known will be investigated." That shut it down.

When it comes to life's calamities I seem to have gone through one of each, and the day a man ever lays his hand on me violently again is the day I will learn how to shoot.

The sad thing is, as a single parent, your love tank is always empty when you don't realize God's love for you. So you reach for someone to love you and although the l-word is tossed around like trash in the breeze, I find myself hating the word in a relationship. "Don't tell me you love me, show me you love me," I told the gay ex husband once. He looked like he'd been slapped. Well? It was an over-used, under demonstrated word too much too often so I am not fond of it.

He even came up to me and hit me in the back between my shoulder blades for standing up to his evil sister instead of standing up for me. I have no use for anymore spineless ninnies that can't leave Mommy or Daddy or stand up to jerk family members to back their wife. Marriage is the most sacred relationship— you don't marry your family, you marry your spouse. I am happy to stay single rather than ever be alone in a relationship again with no backing. Who needs a backstabbing two face as as a spouse?!

With much affection,

Mom

_____

_____

_____

"If you want God's help—keep it holy."—Your Gramma
K

"The eyes of the lord range throughout for those whose
hearts are completely His." 2 Chronicles 16:8 (HSCB).

June 10th, 2020

Dear Riley;

I remember when they gave you Risperidone and you
said you could finally sleep. It was like you were given
back a piece of your life. But oh the side effects! That
drug can make men grow breasts and lactate.

You were raised to take natural remedies over
medication and to think outside the box and stand
outside the crowd. To rebel against societal norms and
go against the majority. In plain words, I raised you
to raise sh––. Just not always against me.

Today was a droopy day. The over-cast sky matched
the inner clouds and I carried them all day unsure
of why. Some days are like that.

I live everyday waiting for the phone call that you have
done something horrific and are in jail or lipped off
the wrong person and got dead. A human train wreck
collides with another human train crash eventually.
I pray for the faith to exchange the negative prophecy
for a positive one. I will wait instead for the call that
means you have changed your mind about me.

You cannot help another until you have helped yourself. That's how I know you aren't ready to be a social worker. I pray you get the help you need in that faulty system you seek to represent rather than utilize.

Love, Mom

_____

_____

_____

"...a man's worst enemies will be those of his own family."
Matthew 10:36 (GNB).

June 11th, 2020

Dear Riley;

When I wrote this journal, I could still tuck you into the pages and revisit you once a day. Now that I am typing it before I send it out to the publisher, I feel an upcoming, pending sense of loss. What happens once I release the document? Is that then the lid of the casket I must close at last? Will someone please tell me how to grieve the undead?!

It's getting harder and harder to know what to say to you. Maybe that is sign of closure, although from my counselling perspective, closure is highly over rated. It is just a resigned acceptance of what is.

These days I feel like I am drowning in life and you're part of the flood. Or am I in high tides without a moat or boat...

Recently I read a great book by Penelope Russianoff;

"When Am I Going To Be Happy? And she says to always try and find three possible explanations for everything.

I have said of romance; "I don't want to be the only log on the river a man is drowning in," And it is true, but

I don't know anyone who would want to volunteer to drown/suffocate/asphyxiate in my current situation either. I think though, that the right man would say; "hey...I'd rather dodge bullets with you than sit in a protected tower alone."

Remember also; "if you spot it you've got it," "it takes it to know it," "whatever you say, that's what you are." Three fingers are pointing back at you for every finger you point.

When you were still in elementary school you developed a penchant for hanging around absolute shmucks. Delinquents. You and a biker's kid named Angel who was anything but were inseparable for a while. The shenanigans were relatively harmless; rolling in mud and ruining your second hand clothes but annoying as all get out. Lol.

Anyway, it's time to put a hard day to rest. I shall go curl up with a sleeping pill and 110 pound Rottweiler as per usual. I have the bedtime of an eight year old, lol.

Love, Mom

"An unhealed person can find offence in pretty much anything someone does.

A healed person understands that the actions of others has absolutely nothing to do with them.

Each day you get to decide which one you will be."—Unknown

June 12th, 2020

Dear Riley;

The other day I found myself praying; "Lord, fill me everywhere my parents left me empty." And you will have to do the same.

Maybe you will blame me for the rest of your life for your problems but you are doing so well so how do you explain that?!" As if I "gots the powah." That is toxic thinking and behaviour; blaming, fault finding; accusing and assuming rather than asking.

Yesterday I bought a wedding dress in case of emergency. Ha ha. Lol. Right? Just like there's chocolate in the first aide kit for emergencies. Well? You're talking to a woman who once went Christmas Caroling right out of the oil change page of her Toyota Camry. Sang it sober and deliberately off-key too. Lol.

It was another stormy day. Methinks the weather
doth eavesdrop on my life and go accordingly.

Love, Mom

_____

_____

_____

"I have seen what a laugh can do. It can transform almost unbearable tears into something bearable, even hopeful."-Bob Hope

June 13th, 2020

Dear Riley;

And the truth about that quote up there is reinforced in John 8:36(NIV); "So if the Son of man sets you free you will be free indeed." When the good Lord set me free of the latest relationship pain I laughed as hard as I had once cried and people can think Bipolar Disorder all they want, I said "Ich bin german, vee isht vay prasht dat."

I remember how when you were 2-3 when I said "okay, let's go," you would say "I have to get organdized." Lol.

This week Rachel will bury her father, they said it is a matter of days now. The cancer is moving fast so they are moving him to La Crete while he is still alive because that is apparently a rule. How grim that palliative patients die alone because of this corona virus. Anyway I made my peace with God about him, so my thoughts and so on wouldn't prevent him from going to heaven. If it works that way-I heard one perception that we can actually prevent ourselves and the person we are mad at from going to heaven with lack of forgiveness. I hope not.

There was a time after years of abuse, stalking, harassment and more that I wanted to pee on his grave. Your dads too. But I took it to Big Daddy and He handled it from there. I don't think thoughts and feelings in themselves a crime or a sin, it is what you do with them that counts.

Be grateful for the time you did have with your pop. That is what I told Rachel too. Some children are given up for adoption and never meet their parents. I heard a lady aged seventy plus say; "all I ever wanted to do is see my mother from across the street to see if I resembled her." Wow huh. Talk about impoverished.

Be grateful. If we all received what we truly have coming because of sin we would all be grease stains on the sidewalk. Thanks to Jesus Christ of Nazareth we are getting far better than we deserve. Always.

Love, Mom

_____

_____

_____

"No one can throw me under the bus anymore—I just park there."—Me

June 14th, 2020

Dear Riley;

Yesterday your sister said something that wrecked me twice over. It's a good thing I can walk on a broken heart. She said; "Mom, dad won't be at my wedding to give me away." And I couldn't fix it. Here you are both grown women and I could not fix it like I want to. So I told her to carry a framed photo up the aisle, and that he lives on in her because she is half him, and that if I know him he was well he will find a way to be there. She said yes she had many relatives and her friend C's dad would walk her up also. I also mentioned how a woman doesn't actually need someone to walk her up and give her away if she isn't owned in the first place?!

I am sorry I could not be there for you in the passing of your father because of your insistence on our estrangement. I am sorry you think you were a victim in our relationship when the truth is, you could piss off a statue and always pushed the envelope and entire office desk. This all ends when I finish the book—no more reminiscing about these negatives. My life is worth as much as yours and I am taking it back.

Your father rejected you twice and cut you off both those times, so I really don't agree that he was the better parent. He was the French-Aboriginal side of you and that is your true issue; racism and hatred. You hate me because I am Caucasian and I am the blockade to you being a full-blood Native. Even though he wasn't a full blood either—is anyone anymore?! He could grow quite a Van Dyke Beard—a sign of white blood in an aboriginal. The truer the Indian the less body hair.

You carry poison and hope it kills everybody else but it's inside of you, so be even smarter than you look and figure out who you are really hurting. Yourself.

Love, Mom

_____

_____

_____

"Few are those who see with their own eyes and feel with their own hearts." -Albert Einstein

"There is a reason God gave us each a brain." -Grandma K

June 15th, 2020

Dear Riley;

I pray one day, real soon, you will see yourself through God's eyes; a human sinner, yet so loved.

I can't remember who it was that said; "we are going to high-tech ourselves right back to the stone age."

It is a sheer disappointment to see the vast majority have lapped up f---book as a good thing. I remember when an entire church was dedicated to the leadership seated on the stage to answer questions during open mike about the internet. I got up and walked out and I didn't give two frigs who noticed either. I wasn't created to be a mindless sheep.

The cyber-world has brought much evil, let alone social media. It enabled men to locate other lovers and cheat on their spouses. Hackers can access everything, and there is virtually no security. Mental health is negatively impacted by social media. I could go on and on. They can name the next country song after me; "The Rambler." Or I sometimes look in the mirror, see the aging and say, "well, if I was a country music star I guess they'd have to call me Myrtle Haggard," lol.

Love, Mom

_____

_____

_____

"Don't piss on my neck and tell me it's raining." —Unknown

"Woe to those who call evil good and good evil, who put darkness for light and light for darkness, who put bitter for sweet and sweet for bitter." Isaiah 5:20 (NIV)

June 16th, 2020

Dear Riley;

I saw my flash temper on yesterday's entry. Wowsers. Emotions have been going roller coaster since I went off medications that threatened to make me fat, lol. All three of us females are so weight conscious.

Do you have days of all out creativity and days of stilted magoo-only moments? Arrgh. Today I couldn't build a second greeting card.

You said in one your 80 thousand hate emails that I was an uneducated _____. I always loved to learn new things and still soak up new information. Student loans never EVER were enough and came through so late by the time I cashed them in total distress I had given up and needed them to pay bills. An accumulation of bills.

I fought with your prop to get you that Native Status Card that will pay for a hundred years of schooling. Plus you get funding out of my pensions, which resulted in the comments: "you're a fraudulent _____." Nice.

What one gets used to from you. Tick-tock said the Karma clock.

I have to let God do my forgiving for me. Sometimes I have to say: "God, I'm willing to forgive." And then the other trick is to be willing every time the thoughts come. Seven times seventy. Yup. Trouble is I "can't math but my english is gooder." I always say that.

Love, Mom

_____

_____

_____

"Look to the one who does not avoid our suffering but enters it in, who does not despise our brokenness but redeems it."—Godly Grief

June 17th, 2020

Dear Riley;

It takes no special talent for one human being to violate another, thanks to human nature. The thought helps me forgive also, especially with a repeat offender like yourself. ALL have sinned.

Make no mistake, a restraining order is not off the table yet, but not for revenge, for practicality. If I receive a barrage of hate emails again.

Today when I prayed for you two girls I specifically asked for you to come back the Lord and not to a church or to me necessarily. Spirituality happens best outside of confined spaces, we just need to gather to share our experiences. My opinion, after countless burn sessions from Churchianity.

Not much has to happen to set me off crying, thanks to grief and C.P.T.S.D. In the eyes of carnal souls, people who are experienced and/or damaged like me are worth less. But God doesn't think like that. Jesus said: "I didn't come for the sinless and the perfect—they have no need of me. There is nothing I can do for them. No, I came for the sick, the maimed, the blind, the lost, the hopeless." (Luke 19:10, loosely paraphrased by me).

Ruined lived are why He died on Calvary. Yay me. I'm in.

Love, Mom

_____

_____

_____

"Don't let your loyalty become slavery. If they don't like what you bring to the table, let them eat alone."–Unknown

"Don't complain when the garbage takes itself out."–Me, on rejection, although paraphrased from Instagram

June 18th, 2020

Dear Riley;

Remember a cubic zirconium is worth almost nothing because it is perfect. A diamond gains value for its imperfections. The more the better. There's a lesson there.

One of my jobs gave me a gym membership. Woo hoo. I will soon be a mixture of muscle over flab. Contents have settled during shipping and handling. You were part of that.

I hope you and Rachel both have kids that act like you did. They say grandchildren are a parents best revenge. HAH. Not that I suffer, I experience. And on their graduation from high school I hope they give a speech that includes: "if it wasn't for Daddy I don't know where I would be–" and then in lieu of my sympathy you can look up the word in the dictionary it's between sh-- and syphilis.

It is a trauma to the body to have children. Then to have them grow up and turn on you like you never mattered, it's a painful experience.

It's getting to be "in masks we trust," not "in God we trust." Society is chalk full of mindless sheep that need the government and social media to tell them what to think next. Pathetic!

I have lovingly revised the serenity prayer: help me to accept what I cannot change which is almost nothing without your power and definitely not other people, the courage to change what you have predestined for me to change—mostly myself; and the wisdom to see a waste of time coming and divert my energy from it; back toward accepting what I cannot change. It really is a full circle. Amen. To summarize; my new mantra is Zechariah 4:6(NIV)...'not by might, nor by power, but by my spirit,' says the Lord Almighty.

I am kind of pleasantly surprised this covid shutdown hasn't turned someone into a water-tower sniper. It is reefing on all our nerves harshly.

Love, Mom

"Behind every jerk is sad story."—Unknown

June 19th, 2020

Dear Riley;

Rachel's dad passed away a few hours ago, within hours of my letter of forgiveness to him and to myself. I let her read it and then I will give her a copy to slip into his casket. Someone tried to be funny and asked me; "did you include a flashlight?"

I decided against going although I left it to Rachel to decide. I didn't want to be in the face of his family who was already burying their king, really. I don't represent a positive to them given how our relationship was...yet I wanted to be there for Rachel. You can already tell grief is occurring. She is randomly very testy and then in the next moment her usual self, then it's; "I can't talk right now."

Do you suppose your fathers met on the other side? I always thought, before forgiveness, that someone should lock them up in a room with only one beer between them. Rachel vehemently said NO to the idea of them having met.

God would have wanted me to give me children in better circumstances, but I say there is no accidental human being. When I said "don't complain when the garbage takes itself out," I didn't mean God made junk, but there sure is some ick behaviour in people.

It's complicated grief for me, grieving your fathers. You girls seem to forget I knew them long before you did? And it is extra hard to hear "daddy was so wonderful, he was my hero," when daddy never had to be the bad guy, daddy only had to show up when it worked for him and it was the same with child support payments. Convenient fatherhood. I was the bad cop, drawing the line, although not enough by the sounds of things.

Did you know even good things cause stress? A wedding and a funeral have the same effect on people. Good stress is called Eu stress. How I long for my jaw to drop from the positive traumas, lol.

A verse I cling to is Job 2:25 (NIV). "I will repay you for the years the locusts have eaten—the great locust and the young locust, and the other locusts and the locust swarm—my great army that I sent among you."

My hair is falling out. It is from the trauma of December 15th, 2019 and the events around that—it's also from the lithium they glued my fractured soul back together with has been trying to put a pot-gut on me also. Fun and games.

Love, Mom

_____

_____

_____

June 20th, 2020

Dear Riley;

I haven't prayed for or about you as much lately but there is such a thing as letting God work in peace.

Ever notice how "churchianity" breeds some of the biggest jerks you know? The most proud, phony, judgmental people I know are religious pharisees and the nicest people I know are spiritual. Now especially that churches are open and closed, "churchian" behaviour like pretending to care for someone is gone because there is no audience to act in front of.

Then there's the coffee mug that says "when God created men she was only joking." Gasp. That ought to turn a long-faced legalist into a tail spin. God is a man! Hence why men can't do wrong. No wonder there are so many jerks in the world—why change when you don't have to? The world makes excuses for "creatures with reachers."

You should have been there when there was a discussion one "Bible study" night and the book "The Shack," came up and gasp—it paints God as an interchanging being that becomes our mother if needed. The church has some way to go on acting on the equality that Jesus taught. I am not sitting silent whilst women are knocked. It really burns my butt when women throw women in front of the bus to survive their childhood and marriage with a misogynist. And church.

I am so exhausted it feels like someone slipped me a roofie. Do you think there's such a thing as relationship burnout? I think I am there. Oh please, pick me.

I still struggle with four letter words...wind rain, snow, and a few others. Ha ha.

Do you have days when you hate your life more than usual or do you love it. Someone once said; "life is never so hard that its impossible to live either." Pretty sure I butchered it but you get the gist?

There is a book polluting my bookcase that will have to be pulled and donated, the author bugs me, climbing in and out of everybody's mind like a tapeworm instead of picking a main one. Complete with run-on sentences. Arrrgh. I grew up in the spelling bee era where you picked a main character to tell your story through.

Love, Mom

_____

_____

_____

"Maturity is learning to walk away from people and situations that threaten your peace of mind, self-respect, values, morals, or self-worth."—Me

June 27th, 2020

Dear Riley;

Today must have been hard for you, it's Father's Day. I just ignore holidays that are imposed on us that mean nothing to me. Why jump up like a programmed rat every time someone says; "celebrate." Or isolate, for that matter. However, God is out ultimate father by creation and hopefully relationship. Why not do something for Him?

I have come to appreciate the word poor, because I prefer to be that way rather than be under a man's thumb cuz ain't none of them ever figured out the true meaning of leadership without dictatorship. A control freak will wither the soul every time. In what universe would the wife of Jesus be made to hang her head in silence because His highness has spoken?! And the Bible says submit to one another...DUH.

It's mutual. Of course most of the drunks and losers I have know have never owned a pot to piss in nor a window to throw it out of, like my uncle would always say. "Too broke to pay attention," he also said. I have no patience to live with a broke-bloke anymore.

Well I want to score a Netflicks feel good movie where good still wins over evil and everyone is reconciled at the end. Or maybe where a couple gets together but it isn't a smooth transition—they learn to love each other. No such thing as perfect love. I went through a Longmire phase, hubba hubba zing zing that hot men on that show. I liked the prickish Aboriginal cop...eye candy you might say. Mostly, I love Walter Longmire's ability to calmly say such damning things to a guilty person.

I tell the Lord, considering the way things are with you it would be no problem sacrificing my firstborn. Well? Most things God asked of us are hard unless with His help...here is one easy thing...and the truth is I kind of have to do that for my survival. I have to give you UP.

"Big Daddy—she is your problem now. Thank you for being her father. Amen."

Love, Mom

_____

_____

_____

"Women are angels. And when someone breaks our wings, we simply continue to fly on a broomstick. We're flexible like that."—Unknown

June 22nd, 2020

Dear Riley;

I can't stand to listen to the song; "Eagle When She Flies," by Dolly Parton. I used to sing it to you when I was pregnant and then after you were born. I found a single CD with that song on it and included it in your goods when I sent them. But it hurts too much to listen to, so maybe I should force myself to because as a counsellor, I would tell people "don't run from your pain. Sit with it. You get rid of pain by feeling it, not by running from it."

"She's a sparrow when she's broken, but she's an eagle when she flies." It's a tribute to women I think, and all the things that are thrown our way to break us but we keep on. Another song I used to sing before Barney was in a scandal was the purple dinosaur's song "I Love You." It went like this: I love you, you love me, we're a happy family, with a great big hug and a kiss from me to you, won't you say you love me too."

Only now it is: "I hate you, you hate me. We're a hateful family with a great big kick in the ass from me to you, won't you sign the restraining order too..."

It isn't that I don't forgive you, and it isn't easy to forgive a repeat offender that will do it again, given the chance. It would be a whole lot easier to forgive someone if they repented and took stock of their own issues. Just saying. If I did not forgive would I be writing to you? Would I somehow still love you if I wasn't walking in forgiveness? I think not.

So my new approach to dandelions is "if it blooms it's not a weed." Therefore it is all good. This has been a good year for them. And with the herbal and healing properties it has...why do we fight so hard to get rid of them?! Roasted Dandelion Root Tea is delicious and I bet the wine made thereof isn't too bad either...

There is a fungal infection in the flower bed from too much rain...lucky me. I have to spray it with some fungicide the neighbour lent me. The joke is; there's covid in the flower garden too.

Love, Mom

_____

_____

_____

"Even the strongest feelings expire when ignored and taken for granted."

June 23rd, 2020

Dear Riley;

Ever notice how you never go to the funeral of an a-type-personality-without-the-organizational-skills?! There. I censored it. No matter how someone might have lived like the devil they died an angel. I disagree. People could at least say: he or she struggled with a-b-c, or something like that.

I dread watching the funeral of D, he was the family/cult leader, even "born-again christians," looked to him before they looked to God it seemed. But I also want the issues to go in the hole with him and be gone so...

You can't get unconditional love from a conditional human being. Pinch off our air supply and we're done.

Tammy Wynette puts it well in her song: "You Hurt The Love Right Out of Me." I am somewhat of a human jukebox.

A.D.H.D. Runs thick in our family, beware. Rachel seems to have it and so do I. The alphabet seems to hate me especially, with having C.P.T.S.D. and symptoms of O.C.D.; probably all 26 letters in no particular order.

Some of us admit things, the rest go on pretending to be okay.

Have you learned terms like "crazy making behaviour," and "Silent Knight," abuse. They along with financial abuse, seem to be the lesser talked about aspects of domestic abuse.

As far as I am concerned, a man who feigns not ever understanding you to keep you explaining your soul is draining your energy so you won't have any to leave with. A man who forces you to go to work because he refuses to support you or won't let you take a job when you want to is a financial abuser.

Anyway now I fell like I am following white rabbits so I will quit before I fall down the hole.

Love, Mom

_____

_____

_____

"God sets the lonely in families, he leads out the prisoners with singing; but the rebellious live in a sun scorched land." Psalm 68:6(NIV)

June 24th, 2020

Dear Riley;

Today I was a miserable b-with-an-itch and have felt rather stuck there. I told myself I didn't really have any daughters for the loyalty and caring I experience from them. It is stinking thinking and inaccurate to boot...Rachel is back after her father's fables turned her against me for a time.

It burns me that your online store is named after a version of the white family last name. After all the hatred you spew about Caucasians.

I am becoming quite the trauma expert from all the counselling I have received plus my own training. It's getting to be so that I can see it on people's faces or smell it on them like fresh paint. When someone looks to their left and appears to be watching a clip that only he can see...that is him trying to figure out trauma from his past. When someone looks to their right past you they are lying. I am a lie detector. I could always tell when you were lying to me which was quite a bit.

Do you remember when us three gals were the Queen of Hearts, A Card, and the white rabbit for that little kids fourth birthday party? She was the precocious daughter of a co worker at the time and our gift to her was the entire set of Laura Ingalls books which her mom said she would be reading before long.

It is nap time for middle aged ladies. You and Rachel once jokingly threatened to put me in a nursing home when I was 45. Ha ha.

Love, Mom

_____

_____

_____

"A survivor of complex trauma may not even know they're traumatized because there wasn't even a single major event. It was their normal."–Unknown

June 25th, 2020

Dear Riley;

There are times I feel so dead inside. Numb. It is normal for a super traumatized person my counsellors tell me. I try not to feel sorry about myself. But sometimes I pray; "if life has to be so bloody unfair, can it be unfair in my favour?!"

Today work consisted of being called to clean a path through a burned out house for the insurance adjusters to be able to walk through and declare it a write off. It was interesting to see how the fire had actually been an energy, moving furniture around. Cleaning a burned house is a different process than a normal one. Like you wash walls bottom to top…this one was so far gone we just shovelled insulation off the floor that had been soaked by the sprinklers. Yuck.

Covid precautions that annoy everyone continue on… it really sounds like pneumonia with a twist. People don't even unfurl their masks all the way and a sneeze can still travel sixteen feet and hit you where you are not masked so what is so special about six feet?! Arrrrgh.

I am a conspiracy theorist...paranoia kind of runs with trauma though.

You traumatize me. Your own mother. But since my hero Jesus forgave the enemies He was dying for as they killed him, I have no reason to say I cannot forgive when He demonstrated it to the uttermost...forgiving people as they insulted and injured Him. I am just not that far yet. It's still a process for me.

Love, Mom

_____

_____

_____

"Someone said 'I'd rather adjust to your absence than be frustrated by your presence.' I felt that." Unknown

June 26th, 2020

Dear Riley;

Today is your Aunt M2's 32nd wedding anniversary. They got married when they were seventeen with nothing between them except a teen pregnancy rumour. Yikes.

I wonder if yours and Rachel's fathers are having a root beer up in heaven, trading stories about me. Play punching Jesus maybe.

The stages of grief are not real organized, even as listed. Anger, denial, bargaining, sadness, acceptance. I think they must be Hodgepodge, and not in any particular order.

The would be father of my first pregnancy is the only one still alive. I must be some kind of Black Widow spider. Only slower.

I feel like all my suffering in poverty and going without while I raised you kids was for nothing. Well, feelings cannot be faulted. On some level, I feel like I have lost all my children at least once.

It rains so much the lawnmower blade now doubles as a propeller on a water wheel. I can't wait for a drying

off period before I cut grass because it is raining
again by then. Pity the poor sucker with the electrical
mower.

Guess what I have to go do. Love, Mom

_____

_____

_____

"Faith makes no provision for failure."—Unknown

June 27th, 2020

Dear Riley;

The periods of blankness over you are growing longer, with memories getting fewer and farther between.

I have said anything can be fixed with God, grace, and guts; ultimately His grace, but at the moment, faith is thin. Or it is the peace I have from God that no matter what happens, He's got us.

The problem with my theory is, I have had relationships that could not be fixed and should not have been. I have had to run for my life and hide in women's shelters. People can judge all they want that I am an overly experienced person in relationships, they haven't fled in my shoes and my shoes would pinch their feet.

Today I got to help save someone's life on the side of highway 20 in the ditch. It felt good.

I gave mouth to mouth resuscitation through a hole in a flimsy sandwich bag because he was not breathing, was turning black and his eyes were rolled back in his head. That part did not feel good—it was gross putting my lips on his cold clammy ones—the baggie kept moving—but once he turned peach and came back it was like woo-hoo. What really did it was my one-word prayer: "Jesus." There were people reefing on his rib cage, that did not do it. Mouth to mouth—it brought him back a few times but he'd fade again. Then I prayed; "Jesus," gave one more breath and he really came back.

Life is about to get busy with full-time work and that is good, because without structure what do you get done.

Zippety. Love, Mom

_____

_____

_____

"Come to me, all of you who are tired from carrying heavy loads, and I will give you rest. Take my yoke and put it on you, and learn from me, because I am gentle and humble in spirit; and you will find rest. For the yoke I will give you is easy, and the load I will put on you is light." Matthew 11:28-30 (GNB)

June 28th, 2020

Dear Riley;

I am running out of things to say to you, yet I wonder what you would have to tell me if you ever get off this vendetta bender.

D is dead and all I feel is nothing. No matter how much you think you love or need someone, it is incredibly incredible how far down the yucca shoot a relationship can go. Did I mention I hate the word love? Because I do.

Now housekeeping clients want me to cut their grass and I tend to break machinery. It is supposed to be an electromagnetic field thing...I wish I had paid attention. The landlord said she has that issue too. So she understood when EVERYTHING in here broke down at least once. You should have seen the self serve checkout thing at Walmart lay down and die today upon my arrival. I can absolutely never, ever use self checkout without a problem. Strap a watch on me and if it doesn't die the strap will. Hee hee.

Lately I have been cashing in prayers, getting lots of answers. It is wonderful, walking closely with God. They say if God feels distant...guess who moved?

Love, Mom

_____

_____

_____

But those who wait on the Lord shall renew their strength; they shall mount up with wings like eagles, they shall run and not be weary, they shall walk and not be faint. Isaiah 40:37 (NKJV)—Unknown

June 29th, 2020

Dear Riley;

That is a good scripture for aboriginals huh? It reminded me of you and the many, many eagles your dad sketched. I hope you have some of his artwork still.

We also used to sing that verse in youth group.

I took the lawn mower to a small business in town that still works out of a recipe box and Que-cards. Cash or cheque only. I have learned to ask how they take payment in H, many folks still do things the old fashioned way. It's an old farming community where you can step outside in town and hear the cows in the feedlot. I love that.

My pets have really helped with the empty nest syndrome. Since their presence makes the nest less empty. Who knew your childhood would end so quickly? It was sixteen for both of you because I couldn't handle the rebellion and what I experienced as betrayal.

God prepared me for your loss a long time ago when I lost Bailey, my first pregnancy. I didn't know it then but He did. Everything that happens He turns around for good, even if it feels like life will only hurt from that moment on. Strength is a good thing derived from absolute agony.

Someone said to me recently about a bad job experience; "they screwed you right up!" I said no, no one is important enough to screw up your life. Nor is anyone big enough to wreck you, besides God. The Bible says: "do not be afraid of those who kill the body but cannot kill the soul. Rather, be afraid of the One who can destroy both body and soul in hell." Matthew 10:28 (NIV). God doesn't actually send people to hell he just honors their choices.

I have learned too that you cannot be cheated, jipped, or robbed of anything or anyone that God wants you to have. Jip is old-speak for cheat or swindle. I guess I just dated myself. Well someone should. Lol.

Love, Mom

_____

_____

_____

"Learn the difference between connection and attachment. Connection gives you power, attachment sucks the life out of you."—Unknown

June 30th, 2020

Dear Riley;

I sometimes worry that you and Rachel might have complicated grief around losing your dads. I mean, you were both the product of a split, you didn't spend a lot of time with them either so you kind of lost your dad twice.

In the psych ward, I went before a panel of professionals every day of the work week and one day I said; "I think I suffer from complicated grief syndrome after the way the hospital stuck me in a room with a woman in labour after I lost my pregnancy. But as soon as I said it something lifted off of me. Secrets are to sickness and openness is to wholeness.

What a ripoff too when someone dies that you have unresolved issues with. That's when you pray and ask God to pass along a message.

The rain is not ceasing. It can do my crying for me today.

Do you remember when you used to like chewing on ice cubes and it would drive me ape — snake — canary —

crackers? It ruins the enamel on your teeth. Well it isn't good for it.

I still don't know what is worse, losing a child to death or rebellion. And part of me really doesn't want to know.

Okay! Experience—not suffering.

When I was in the puzzle-palace I rewrote the words to the country song by Merle Haggard; "Okie From Muskogie," to be "Okie From Ponokie," and the chorus ran like this:

"I'm proud to be an Okie from Ponokie,

a place where everyone has had a fall,

we don't claim no glory at the nuthouse,

and medications not the biggest thrill of all."

Well it is the truth if nothing else.

Love, Mom

_____

_____

_____

"Learn to be done with people. Not mad, not bothered, just done." –Unknown

"If anyone will not welcome you and listen to your words; leave that home or town and shake the dust off your feet." Matthew 10:14 (NIV)

July 1st, 2020

Dear Riley;

Yesterday I got out boxes of old negatives and sorted them a little. I discovered a picture of you and one of Rachel but I couldn't get the convert-a-negative-to-photo-app to work. There are so many! Anyway I wanted to discover any pictures of your fathers I might not have kept other than the film thereof and have them developed to give you, but I couldn't find them.

Then I remembered what a giver you were as a young child, always making things and thrusting them into people's hands. Or a Christmastime you gathered your own personal belongings to re-gift to people.

I sure wish tossing and turning while trying to sleep counted as exercise. I would finally be an Olympian.

The other day I cancelled my life insurance policy. It's pretty bad when the cost of that practically starves you. And no one owes anyone an inheritance.

In two years you will be 25, and your brain will scientifically be fully matured. I wonder if anything will change.

Today I am going to an MRI to check my brain for damage from all the blows and falls. When I passed out from the suicide attempt I hit the counter on my way down...plus all the other times I fell as a kid or was punched in the face. I probably need not worry, I am a German. The helmet is built in. Ha ha.

Love, Mom

_____

_____

_____

"We don't develop courage by being happy every day. We develop it by surviving difficult times and challenging adversity." -Barbara De-Angelis.

July 2nd, 2020

Dear Riley;

Just how much adversity is finally enough is what I would love to know.

I continue to pray rough prayers for you...for God to get through to you, to stop your tirade of hate and tangent of racism. Maybe legal trouble is your best bet to seeing the light, make that flashing lights if need be.

Do you remember when you told me I was a horrible f-ing mother and in the same breath asked for two hundred dollars for grad photos? I said "sorry, rotten parents ride for free." I thought that was a good one.

Walking with God is not an option when you live overwhelmed. I guess PTSD has its perks.

Do you know a domestically abusive man will refuse to so much as arm wrestle on a good day? Until he loses control completely and then it is much more than an arm wrestle.

Recently, one of the prickly people from a local cult said to me "I think finding a man is too much a priority in your life." I said "you don't know my life." When you are utterly alone in the universe except for friends that make those type of comments, yikes. When your family always treats you like an outsider and gangs up on you, your only hope for love and family is a romance and in laws, or a church family, but what a joke that has been. Joke that never turned funny. Forgiveness never changed my story yet and I don't know why it would.

Love, Mom

_____

_____

_____

"Your anointing is greater than your opposition."—
Joel Osteen

July 3rd, 2020

Dear Riley;

I regret all the time I missed with you and Rachel because
of men, a sleeping pill addiction at one point, leaving
you alone for short periods of time to go back alley beach
combing for furnishings for our house that people were
throwing away. Typical addict—love someone so much
you run from them. There were other reasons too like
having to work and having to sleep off graveyard shifts.

They say grandchildren are a grandparents revenge
but I pray against them until the time is absolutely
right.

There are no notes in with the gift stash for you. I
included a lot of notes with the two apple crates when
I sent your baby stuff but I am distancing myself and
when there is no relationship there is not much to say.

I have lamented to the Lord; "my kids have crucified
me!" He said "yeah I know the feeling." Does He ever!"
Big Daddy has the same kind of kids we do, rebellious,
ungrateful, betraying, and more.

Love, Mom

_____

_____

"The Lord your God is among you, a warrior who saves. He will rejoice over you with gladness. He will be quiet in his love. He will delight in you with singing." Zephaniah 3:17 (CSB).

July 4th, 2020

Dear Riley;

I am trying to quit Covid but there is not much cooperation. Everyone I talk to is sick of it even if not sick with it. This is going to cause P.T.S.D. in people.

I keep telling myself every negative thing ends up a positive-in algebra two negatives make a positive. There you go every two crappy incidents make a good one.

We are all cutting grass in the rain, throwing grass clippings and water droplets alike. Pity the poor bloke with the electric mower, lol. There is a fungicide in my flower bed-probably the corona virus also, ha ha. It is from too much rain.

A good scripture I cling to is: "if we are faithless, He remains faithful, for He cannot disown Himself.." 2Timothy 2:13.(NIV) Kind of the same as the promise "I will never leave you or forsake you."

Love, Mom

_____

_____

_____

"You may write me down in history

with your bitter, twisted lies

You may trod me in the very dirt

but still dust, I'll rise."—Maya Angelou poem, Still I Rise

July 5th, 2020

Dear Riley;

Today is your Grandparents 50 the wedding anniversary. It got to be a real habit.

It is also Independence Day in the states. It is also as good a day as any to close the books cover and the lid on your coffin.

I know you are not dead literally but I have decided that death is easier to deal with.

Thanks to being a believer in Jesus, I have the luxury of both lowering the lid and raising hope. At the very least, the past has to be put to death for us to have a resurrection of sorts for our relationship. So I finally found my way out of the gloom, emphasis; my way. To each their own.

Even death for real isn't as final as it feels for a spiritual person, because there is a spiritual life that continues. We don't end, we evolve.

I am leaving the funeral parlour now, exhausted, but holding my head high and shucking my black outer garments and veil.

This will not hurt anymore because I choose not to suffer any longer. I am moving on as I have been, with the casket closed and my eyes clear of tears and free of the sorrow you caused.

I hope no one judges me for how I choose to handle this, but I do not care. This is my journey after all.

I am still your mother. I love you. I forgive you. I forgive myself, and I hope one day you will too. Good bye. Good bye.

—Mom

_____

_____

_____

Manufactured by Amazon.ca
Bolton, ON